200

D1250431

THE
FUTURE
OF
UNBELIEF

THE
FUTURE
OF
UNBELIEF

by Gerhard Szczesny

Translated from the German by Edward B. Garside

GEORGE BRAZILLER
New York 1961

First Printing

Library of Congress Catalog Card Number: 60-11665

Printed in the United States of America

What can be said at all, can be clearly said; of that which eludes utterance, best say nothing.

—WITTGENSTEIN

CONTENTS

1. *The Genesis of These Reflections*   11

2. *Transitional Epochs—Times of False Orientation*   19

3. *Christianity, an Early Theology Perpetuated*   27

4. *The Psychological Grounds for Europe's Conversion*   57

5. *Christianity's Creative Promise Unfulfilled*   71

6. *The Period of Ersatz Religions*   85

7. *Notes on the Theme of Objectivism*   97

8. *Notes on the Theme of Subjectivism*   111

9. *Simplicity of Reason and Artistry of the Spirit*   123

10. *From Physics to Metaphysics*   137

11. *The Three Pillars of Unreason*   151

12. *Humanity as a Natural Event*   169

13. *The Duty to Be Unholy and Unwise*   195

14. *By Way of Conclusion*   213

THE
FUTURE
OF
UNBELIEF

1

THE GENESIS OF THESE REFLECTIONS

THE EVENTS OF the first half of our century certainly have not led to a renascence of the Christian faith. They have, however, brought about a revival of the secular currency and authority of Christianity. After the failure of recent substitute religions, Christianity again seems like the unassailable treasure house of all human values. The writings of a David Friedrich Strauss, a Ludwig Feuerbach or a Friedrich Nietzsche, if published today, in all likelihood would be greeted as a public scandal and give rise to parliamentary protest by all "Christian" parties. We are faced by the fact, a fact in many respects historically and psychologically explainable, yet on the whole still extraordinary, that the argument with Christianity which began more than a hundred years ago has in recent decades become increasingly taboo.

One of the reasons for this phenomenon is the collapse of the intellectual and moral optimism that was the mark of the century past. As opposed to a simple, pristinely joyous belief in life, Christianity proved itself to be a richer and deeper thing. It knew more of the unavailingness of all human striving and the need always to take this frustration into account. Finally, it knew more about man's inclination to turn to the mysteries, to form some notion of what lies beyond the rationally knowable.

This rediscovery and reawakening of Christianity as a universally binding moral institution has not, to be sure, altered the fact that the real content of the Christian doctrine of salvation, for a dominant type of modern man, has become completely unacceptable, indeed, a matter of indifference. Intelligent Christians admit this without hesitation. However, in the face of modern crises and catastrophes the security afforded by a venerable and firmly built structure of belief makes Christianity, as a whole, taboo and hinders open critical analysis of it, even of its now unbelievable metaphysics. Thus, existing Christian dogma, which possesses social currency even while no longer seriously believed, obstructs that looking out and beyond needed to find new answers to the "final questions."

Our inquiry in this direction is not undertaken with any intention of making apostates of Christians. It is rather concerned with those to whom "unbelievingness" has become habitual, and from whom a return to Christianity can no longer be expected. It is aimed at overcoming the illusion that the "godless" man is an inferior creature, a nihilistic form of existence making for the total ruination of all human order—in sum, an utterly devilish sort of apparition the fighting of which with every means at hand demonstrates insight, humanity and adherence to the Christian way. This book is anti-Christian only in its contention that such views are enjoined or promoted, that there is a recognizable proclivity to bring the non-Christian standpoint into disrepute and to put social, moral and political pressure to bear on those who embrace it. Otherwise this book is no more intended to be anti-Christian than anti-Taoist or anti-Anthroposophic. It will defend the freedom of Christians to profess their beliefs and practice their form of worship. But it will equally defend the rights of those who have non-Christian forms of conviction and modes of behavior. And precisely on this account it will repudiate Christian claims to cultural or political dominion.

The sharpness of many ensuing formulations is conditioned not by the subject matter itself, but by the situation surrounding the subject matter. The author is neither a backslider nor a protester, nor any sort of anti- or pro-religionist. He respects Christianity as a world-shaking historical manifestation, which has left its mark for two thousand years. But Christianity as a confession of faith he does not respect. The author is also well aware that many people who cling earnestly and honestly to Christianity are people of good will and good faith. It is not easy for him to wreak injury on his friends among such Christians. But under present circumstances he sees no way of taking up the cause of the "unbelievers" without at the same time putting the patience and open-mindedness of the believers to a severe test. Any reader who considers this to be asking too much may as well lay the book aside at once. But anyone who, as a Christian, decides to hear the author out, might bear in mind that everybody denied the gift of "belief" can hardly, on that account, abandon all thinking about the world and the role he plays in it, and how these are to be understood.

The following observations represent random thoughts on the relationships between Christianity and modern crises in belief, rather than a systematic analysis. They also represent an attempt to characterize the typical content of a post-Christian ideology or world-outlook. Among these random thoughts appear certain remarks on this great family of problems which assume a solution in a certain direction. Yet in no wise are they to be understood as final or comprehensive. Our task is to throw light on the basic, root question of diversity of viewpoint. Certain trains of thought will recur again and again, since they establish a connection between the widely disparate objects of our analysis. Many things in the following pages may appear trivial. But it is the fate of certain truisms that whereas everyone knows them, no one really pays them the least attention. There are commonplaces which, if publicly expressed, arouse resentment. They are allowed to hold good only as long as no one brings them to mind. This is understandable. The bad conscience of our epoch not only makes for complicated illusions, but for downright suppressions as well.

This observer's platform, then, is nothing more than the usual vantage from which the normal man of our times occasionally tries to cast a look at the great context of his life. "Unbelief" is no longer the prerogative of an especially enlightened minority. It is the fate of a contemporary type of Western man who may actually be in the majority, or who at any rate is very frequently encountered. This contemporary normal man is concerned with the old basic questions: Who am I? What is the nature of the world? What can I believe in and what must I do about it? It is hard to find answers to these questions in the field of learning appropriate to their consideration. Without wishing to belittle the significance of modern philosophy, one must recognize the fact that its contributions toward resolving the spiritual crises of our time are small indeed. On the one hand the philosophers wear themselves out making ever more refined interpretations of handed down conceptual systems. On the other, their voice never reaches beyond a small circle of initiates to those who might profit by philosophy's answers or solutions. Christianity's claim to spiritual leadership, its fear of the "ideological" and the murkiness of its own terminology seal the self-chosen or guilt-born apartness of Western philosophy. The implicit and unsettled conflict with the

Christian metaphysic lies like mildew over all the philosophers' effort to show us how the innermost world is made. Also, the way our school philosophers write, their very style has always served more to cloud than to clarify and continues to do so to this day. The European's specific "intellectual gift" is to think and argue. Yet this gift, in all probability, is largely intelligible as nothing more than the product of a centuries-old clash with theology, in the course of which the art of concealment, evasion and deception has been consummately developed. But a philosophy that can function only under camouflage and proviso eventually loses clarity of insight and impartiality of judgment. In consequence, the day finally arrives when it can produce nothing but the ambiguous and equivocal.

In all events, the average modern man—and by this we mean the average "educated" man—must manage his life, its problems and tragedies, without benefit of advice from our professional thinkers. There is also reason to suspect that as soon as these people have to measure up to the fundamental questions of human existence outside their bookish province, they, too, will behave in a "dilettante" and naïve fashion. Anyone who has ever listened in on a discussion among philosophers, or a discussion in which philosophers took part, will have noted with astonishment that at decisive moments in the debate they abandon the well-traveled paths of their specialized fund of knowledge and, like any other mortal, at best can utter only subjective, perplexed and simple opinions on God and the world. Actually this is a gratifying thing. At the bottom, to philosophize simply means a direct attempt to read meaning into the nature of things, not spinning thoughts about other thoughts and writing another book about other books.

Therefore, since here what we have in mind is a direct interpretation of the modern situation rather than another contribution to academic philosophy, we shall give up all dependence on documents, writings and citable names to prop our argument. Very little or nothing will be taken for granted. For it must be possible to develop out of raw experience a line of thought that will be accessible to everybody, and to develop it in such fashion that everybody can follow it through. What does it profit us to drag in the name of this or that author, however prominent, if we are not in a position to explain the reference we have in mind in our own words? And would it make our thesis any more enlightening or true if we took refuge behind the authority of some philosopher whose authority, meanwhile, was being questioned by still other authorities?

Our deliberations go straight to the heart of the matter. The world in which we find ourselves offers such aspects as these: birth and death, old age and sickness, happiness and misery, the results of man's scientific insight into nature and into himself. Thus a picture of relationships is generated, and a need to interpret the picture. In this manner what is known as a "Weltanschauung," an ideology, a way of looking at the world, comes into being.

As a word and concept "Weltanschauung" has fallen into disrepute since it was taken over by the propagandists of the new German barbarism. Nevertheless, we feel we cannot dispense with it. The word as such stems neither from Marx nor Haeckel nor Hitler. It was discovered by the Romantics and popularized by Wilhelm Dilthey. And no one was ever less materialistic or trite than he. The word "Weltanschauung"—a way of viewing the world intuitively arrived at—in our opinion more intelligibly expresses the common human need for a comprehensive interpretation of all existence, within reason's grasp and beyond it, than does the word "religion." So thoroughly is the term "religion" steeped in Christian notions of faith and Christian emotional values that it has become virtually unusable except to connote a specifically Christian form of man's response to the cosmos. A restoration of the discredited concept of "Weltanschauung" to its original worth seems possible to us. It can be done if "Welt" (world) is understood as containing everything in the cosmos, known and unknown. Beyond this, "Anschauung" (contemplation) must refer to an intuitive as well as a rational apprehension of the aforementioned totality.

Actually everything that will be said in this book could be couched in terms of an interpretation of both concepts, "religion" and "Weltanschauung" (hereafter, in English, world-outlook or ideology). If "religion" seems to us to be something larger, deeper and more inclusive than mere "ideology," at the same time we are aware that we still harbor a secret wish to fashion our own way of regarding the world, and one which will have no connection with what in this country is called "religion." With this the stage is spiritually and psychologically set for our deliberations.

2

TRANSITIONAL EPOCHS—
TIMES OF FALSE ORIENTATION

THE DECADES, NOW beginning to fade into the past, which comprised the lives of our parents and grandparents, were a remarkable period, filled with glitter and glory, of unheard of accomplishments and of unheard of degradations as well. People of this epoch named it the "modern" period. They had a very positive feeling of being separated by a great gap from preceding generations. In their self-confidence and challenging pride they fancied themselves to be independent, unique and advanced in all respects. They believed they were seeing the revolutionary dawn of an era of new values, a new human condition. This belief has proved illusory. Modernity was not so much the beginning as the end of an era. It was a time of transition, replete with astounding errors and the most frightful misachievements.

The modern era was an end indeed. It marked the last uneasy phase of the Christian faith's waning creative power. It was the

sentimental Indian summer of a millennium of autocratic spirituality. It also saw the ominous fall of a century of bold trust in
reason. Yet at the same time it was a beginning of a godless era,
of a reduction to conformity of all forms of life and knowledge.
Of a period, catastrophically dawning, of inescapable historical significance.

A century in which such opposed trends intersect becomes of
necessity an epoch of false perspectives, of self-destructive pessimism and arrogant pride, of individual and mass neuroses of all
description. Still housed in the old structure of belief, still given
over to the forms of living and intuiting of a no longer convincing
world scheme, the old and the new of this "time between times"
conflict and interweave in a great confusion. Meanwhile, in anger
and bitterness, some take their stand on the old, hoping, by repairing the crumbling façade, to effect a renewal of traditional values.
Still others strive to synthesize the old spirit and the new, by at-
tempting to fit old content into new forms, or new content into
old ones. Opposed to both are the heralds of the coming age. These
people either exhaust themselves in a total denial of the status quo,
or, ignoring the whole sphere of things inherited, keep busy carrying
out all manner of new discoveries.

Thus everything comes into false relationship and takes on a
false tone. Meanwhile the old world image is still officially in force
and deeply rooted in human thought and feeling. In consequence
fresh misunderstandings and conflicts steadily arise. At every hand
completely alien structures come to interpenetrate and overlay each
other. The still-binding social order is contrary to the natural sense
of what is right. Customary political forms are no longer adequate
to contain the peoples' technical and social development. Even
as he strives for full autonomy man remains largely subject to feudal
and authoritarian conventions. The monist and dynamic world-

picture of the new sciences stands opposed to a dualist and static metaphysics.

The most serious and dangerous result of this situation is the fact that when the content of the old, religious world-image is lost, lost with it are all other world-images that might provide an all-inclusive means of intuiting and interpreting the phenomena of existence. The old dogmas still dominate the "religious" with such natural-ness and authority that the contemporary individual who ignores or denies them loses sight of the whole religious experience, and either tries to disavow its significance or replaces it with other and inadequate elements. The field of vision narrows down to partial contexts. Man makes an "ideology" out of anything and everything that momentarily fascinates him. Thus a period rich in substitute religions comes into being. The old shell of belief meanwhile obstructs the view of existence in its total scope and oneness. In the end all orientation is lost.

The consequences of this loss are incalculable. There is a lack of any real point of departure for the creation of an ideology that will interpret meaningfully and regulatively the connection between realms of being which are accessible to reason and those which are inaccessible. Man himself, his spirit, intellect, soul and senses, to-gether with his history, social context and his natural environment as scientifically known—all of these, in succession or all at once, are either over- or undervalued. In all events, they are not seen in terms of obviously productive relationships derived from a single system of metaphysical coordinates. Experiments in interpretation and order-giving are made which, thanks to their false evaluation of all aspects of life, repeatedly lead to crises and catastrophes. Demagogues gain control of the faith-seeking masses and moral values are increasingly sacrificed to the fanaticism of ersatz religions. For with the disappearance of religious convictions to determine man's position relative to the cosmos, the ground is cut from under his ethical position. Since humanity's old foundations are no longer believed in, doubt arises about the need for any moral behavior at all. What sense is there in obeying commands issued by a dead god, or one who may never have existed at all? Moral nihilism follows in the wake of ideological nihilism. Ersatz religions artificially created to overcome this nihilism set up their own tablets of command and raise half- and quarter-truths to the status of law. Everything is deemed good which appears useful to the soul, the body, the individual, the collectivity, the preservation of tradition or the acceleration of progress.

Abuses appear as a result of this lack of ethical orientation which give rise to loud cries for a new and genuine human outlook on the world. At this juncture the old faith, still current and powerful, offers itself as a means of deliverance. What could be more apparent than the thesis that salvation from the imminent collapse of all spiritual, moral and cultural values lies in a reinstatement of the traditional world-image? Meanwhile, the substitute religions have demonstrated their fateful inability to provide a solution worthy of human dignity. In this fashion begins the phase of restoring the old. The supporters of this movement—who, needless to say, occupy leading positions in the state and in society and who control public opinion—with mounting zeal busy themselves spreading out anew, before the longing gaze of a humanity craving truth and leadership, the riches of the traditional doctrine of salvation. Restorative tendencies triumph in all fields. But the deception inherent in this powerful renascence cannot be long maintained. It soon becomes admitted that all the new partial knowledge and partial perspectives do not add up to an all-embracing world-outlook; on the other hand, to the extent that the new knowledge and perspectives have a partial validity and have become accepted factors in human consciousness, they cannot be incorporated into the world-picture of the old belief. The suppression of new aspects of experience turns out to be as impossible as their amplification into ersatz religions.

The fresh crisis which now takes shape, the crisis after "the return to the good old values," in contrast to the pre-restorative stage of crisis has a distinctly positive tone. The urgent need for a comprehensive world-scheme now has only one way out. This is a forward direction, an approach which goes beyond partial aspects, through them and beyond, rather than merely against them. After the failure of the restorative experiment, no other choice or possibility remains except to hack out a path toward a new truth which will impress unity on the many partial forms of knowledge. The question can no longer be: How, for better or worse, produce a fruitful relation between the ancient creed and new forms of knowledge? It must now be: How go about elevating the experience and knowledge which invalidated the older beliefs, into a world-image which also encompasses the sphere of all that lies beyond human experience and knowledge? And in what light will man's position in the cosmos and his historical task then appear?

A new picture of the world naturally does not take shape over-night as the result of a linear series of reasoned deliberations. It comes, rather, after a long and complicated process of growth, much of it occurring in the unconscious. The experiences and discoveries which first threw doubt on the credibility of the old world-scheme are rooted many generations back. This means that whenever conflict shapes up in the full light of consciousness, a new feeling for the world has already been unconsciously at work. New, scientific truths corresponding to the old truths based on faith at first are only fleetingly and reluctantly registered in consciousness. But they sink down into the subconscious and there gradually give rise to a deep-reaching alteration of the fundamental social mood, this quite independent of all officially binding tenets of faith. As soon as the waking consciousness begins to slough off the overlay of creedal residue, the new feeling toward the world, already tumescent beneath the surface, bursts forth into view. In a situation of this sort limits are imposed upon what, under normal conditions, would be a meaningful demand to continue the past. Old beliefs cannot be indefinitely transposed. The day must come when the discrepancy between old and new becomes too great to be bridged. When this stage of development is reached the old beliefs are dismantled by a revolutionary thought-process and replaced by new ones.

Today we stand at the end stage of the restorative phase of a transition period. The circumstance that conservatively adjusted generations may be expected to dominate for several decades more tends to obscure the fact that the majority of people living today have actually already made the decisive turn. But as time goes on it will become increasingly clear that it is impossible to escape the crisis inherent in a transitional period by flight into the past. This cannot be done politically, morally or "religiously." The inherited metaphysical, ethical and social systems are simply not able to contain, and so cannot shape, the new state of affairs and its peculiar needs. Transitional periods are richer in content than periods of secure conviction and reliable convention, since their purview includes everything which cannot be incorporated into the rigidly determined life-style and picture of the world.

Along with this ubiquitous richness of material ready to be accepted and understood necessarily comes a loss of intensity and depth of insight. The panorama opened up to modern man is studded with ever new attractions. But the key to understanding them is missing. Carried away by a swift succession of shifting impressions, vainly man tries to find a fixed point of reference from which to impose order on the scene. Man presses on and ever on into new realms of nature. He explores the last deserts, mountains and oceans. But all this he does without knowing whence, whither or why. He is robbed of a general view and overall meaning by the dizzy tempo of change, by the profusion of phenomena ceaselessly laying claim to his attention, by the multiplicity of demands on his professional, social and private life. At home in all departments and spheres, he is yet unable really to know or to judge anything. Life slides by him in bright motley, fleetingly, never pausing, like the landscape beneath a plane. Before he has time to make sense out of one particular, the eye is forced to move forward to another one. However, as in a plane the gaze, sliding blindly over many surfaces, suddenly without warning may apprehend the largeness and wholeness of it all, so in times of transition an overpowering sense of security and liberation may suddenly arise, just when it has long been thought forever lost. When this occurs the basic connectedness of a world that had seemingly disintegrated into millions of phenomena and processes stands revealed in a new experience of space and time and a new encounter with being. At these rare moments of spontaneous insight the mystery is lighted up, that very mystery which the religious believe they alone possess and alone can communicate, but in the face of which, in truth, they fail.

Why is it that Christian teaching does not contain the formula for impressing a synoptic meaning on all our modern information and knowledge? Why is it that a light no longer burns amid the darkness? Why is it that Christ's presence does not manifest itself in our deeds, good or bad, in our hope or our despair? Why are we unable, with the best of will, to leap across the unbridgeable abyss which we know separates us from what we should believe? Why do we think of the Bible as pious legend and repository of visions, the poetry of which moves but does not enlighten us?

Anyone who has had ancestral convictions handed down to him, must give a reckoning on this dilemma, to himself and to his contemporaries. A house of faith erected in the passionate conviction and longing for deliverance of generations cannot be used by its inheritors as a sort of hotel or museum to duck in and out of. The world in which these inheritors live has not, in fact, been a Christian world for a long time, though Christianity is still at work in it. It is a challenge to intellectual and moral honesty to take our origins and history seriously, and never more so than at the moment when we are cutting loose from them. We must try to understand that which we can no longer believe in. The freedom to develop a new scheme of existence comes only if we duly respect and understand the creedal notions handed down to us.

3

CHRISTIANITY,
AN EARLY THEOLOGY PERPETUATED

AS WE READ about it, the history of Christianity's spread throughout the Mediterranean and Europe seems remarkable indeed. At the same time we cannot fail to recognize that, as Christ's message to the world arose from a specific religious experience, into being with it came a dogmatic fixation of the understanding of self and the world which, over the long run, has proved incompatible with the European mentality as it developed in quite another manner and direction. The European's innate tendency systematically to investigate the phenomena of his environment and to trace out the objective laws visibly governing nature sooner or later had to lead to irreconcilable conflict with the Christian religion. For though a mighty spiritual force, this religion's basic attitude is anti-objective and on this account it has either ignored or failed to see the immanently binding lawfulness of things.

Christianity claims to be a "world" religion, but originally it was not a world religion at all. The fundamentals of the Christian creed were developed by a people whose historical and geographical situation could hardly be imagined as more endemic, more idiosyncratic in time and space. During the phase of mankind's history when the high religions of Buddhism, Christianity and Islam arose, the cultures out of which they came were still rooted fast, each in its own peculiar and different living-space. The interpretive attempts of these supreme religions sprang from an understanding of the world unmistakably bearing the stamp of a particular landscape, climate and historical destiny. But a real world religion is conceivable only when the humanizing and civilizing process has reached a stage where a world-consciousness free from all cultural specificity and shared by all peoples can take shape. Only now, and for the first time, are we witnessing the tentative beginnings of such a development, one which, as it runs its course, will bring about the extinction of the so-called "high" type of religion. For this type of world construct, being closely bound up with mythic and magic thinking, cannot be separated from a definite culture. Like the culture itself, its psychology is environmentally determined. Similarly, the period of advanced religions will not be succeeded by a period of a one-world religion, but by a period of a one-world ideology.

However, the fact that a religion is taken over from alien peoples, instead of being developed within its own cultural confines, should not be construed as meaning that it can never, in principle, be united with views derived from indigenous experience. Actually a basic incompatibility exists only if the adopted notions of belief prove to be incapable of development and adjustment. However, this happens to be the case with Christianity, and in marked degree. Christianity is the precipitate of a conglomeration of mythic, magical and ideological notions from a variety of folk religions.

Insofar as it is a revealed religion, that is, once and for all tied down to a primitive and inadequate understanding of the world, to this fundamental extent it is incapable of change. Christianity has assumed many forms as it came into contact with different cultures. But always the basic theme persists: a belief in a Creator-God, unbridgeably separated from the world, who once and only once revealed himself to mankind in the historic person of his son, Jesus Christ, through whom mankind can be redeemed from sin and death by belief in him, according to God's boon of faith.

A concept of the world condensed in a myth, that is, in a humanly accessible symbol of significant cosmic and historical events, is not necessarily false and misleading simply because it is a myth. World-images that accord with reality are not differentiated from those that do not by kind and degree of rationalization. It is the scheme and relating system of the mythology, religion, metaphysics or philosophy in question, the means by which the world's content is brought into an intelligible line of sight, that makes the difference. Any modern ideology would itself be naïve, if it presumed, for instance, that the conceptual system in which it was striving to net the world was the only possible and final formulation of truth. But such an ideology could still orient its pronouncements according to the right ground plan and shape its way of viewing to fit the model.

A summary glance through the history of mythologies and religions reveals two basic and divergent types of interpretative systems. On the one hand we find ideas based on the observation of natural events; on the other, those originating out of man's contemplation of his inner self. A people who can grasp the change of the seasons and nature's becoming and passing away have grasped something of the real nature of being. But it is doubtful whether anything of the real, underlying interconnectedness can be appre-

hended when the content of dreams and visions, the ancestral
genealogy or some communal experience is interpreted as a fundamental principle of the world-order. Images arising in fantasy,
dreams and ecstatic states reveal something of what goes on within
the human psyche. But of the way the world is put together they
reveal nothing. They "mean" something. But they do not signify—
as the naïve man supposes—a breakthrough of "true reality." Nor
can a cosmic scheme arise from the social life of a community, or
from the life of an individual reacting within the community.
Schemes of this sort are proper only to the peculiar way and fate
of their origins. Whenever events occurring within an individual, or
within and as part of a community, are carried over to represent
reality's total interdependence, the danger of missing the mark
always exists.

Mankind's early world-images were nourished by both well-
springs, by nature and by personal or communal experience. In both
cases the formulation is anthropomorphic, regardless of whether it
is based on natural events, or on psychic and historical experience.
In the second instance, however, not only the formulation as such,
but the experiential material on which it depends, are both of exclusively human origin. When this occurs, the tie with events of
the world-out-there is broken. With this is lost the possibility of
controlling the objective world and of orienting oneself to accord
with its terms. The decision as to which direction a cosmology will
take can occur at any point in time in a people's history. The assumption now suggests itself that it is prevailing conditions, the
life-situation at a particular time, which generates the decision.
Certain climatic-geographic and historical circumstances appear to
facilitate the evolvement of an understanding of reality marked by
rightness and true correspondence. Others hinder it, and some, so
it seems, make it forever impossible.

The basic elements of the Christian religion stem from a people who, at the time they worked them out, were trapped in an extremely unfavorable life-situation. Indeed, it was precisely because the times were so menacing and hopeless that these notions were developed in the first place. Centuries of enslavement in Egypt, forty years of wandering in the wilderness, the struggle to establish the Jewish kingdoms in Canaan, the Babylonian captivity, the subjugation and eventual dispersion of the Jews by Rome—such were the Jewish people's great stations of the cross. However, their time of decision came during the years of wandering through the desert. On Mount Sinai Yahweh became the god of Israel. It was Moses who covenanted with him and thus salvaged his people's self-esteem, by forcing them to accept inimical fate as a sign of election and a way to grace.

The Jewish people saw themselves as ground down and lost, sacrificed to a destiny that must forever remain closed to human reason and human ideas of justice. There was only one way to endure the willfulness of such a fate: to sanctify this willfulness and then assimilate it into one's own will. Once this was done, Israel's wrathful God not only reflected but justified the Jewish people's hopeless situation after the flight from Egypt.

From this viewpoint fear and misery, slavery and dispersion, are signs of promise. They are proofs that God decrees a hostile destiny in order to demonstrate his promise of later fulfillment to Israel. In this manner, by virtue of their very history, the Jews became God's "chosen people." Whatever may go wrong is not to be thought of as political vicissitude, but as supernatural consideration. The Jewish form of belief is an historical metaphysic. It arises from a conviction of being involved in a train of events which, just because they are so extraordinary and incomprehensible, must by definition connote God's exclusive concern. In sum, the Jews be-

came God's people, a community united and raised above others
by this belief. Having led them out of the wilderness, God would
lead them on to the Promised Land.

This ideological process, unlike some, did not occur gradually
and unconsciously. It was introduced by Moses in one grandiose
act of lawgiving and prophecy. On Mount Sinai Yahweh revealed
himself as Israel's god, and made known to his people what he
expected of them henceforth. The Jewish deity is a highly personal
god. The ground and goal of his decisions are immune to human
understanding, but they are still perfectly concrete decisions. God
is thought of as the personal, autocratic counterpart of the creatures
sacrificed to his will. His subjects' highest virtues are humility and
obedience. Between the Creator-God and his human creation
yawns an abyss. The Jewish idea of God is pure monotheism
and pure transcendence. Only Islam produced a monotheism of
comparable finality. One of the consequences of this personal and
daemonistic idea of God is a readiness to expect the unusual, the
miraculous at any time, whether in shape beneficent or malign. Life
is a concatenation of expressions of God's will, which are taken
as they come, but which can neither be comprehended nor in the
least swayed.

Under such a configuration, only with difficulty can a feeling
for rational political behavior develop. Active participation in
history assumes a belief in history as a human medium, an assumption that social problems can be solved by study and compromise.
Judaism's historical metaphysic bears witness to a lack of clear
sense of historical necessity. It indicates a failure to understand the
fact that history is not something that befalls mankind for reasons
unknowable, but something that comes to pass through mankind.
What makes the Jewish people's relation to history so confusing
and peculiar unto itself is a combination of fervent belief in the

religious meaning of history coupled with a complete lack of understanding of historical interrelationships.

The concept of election, of being a chosen people, the conviction that its history is a special history, has brought Israel, as no other people, into conflict with its environment. This has gone on throughout centuries and millennia, with Israel now amalgamating for a time, now fiercely pulling away. The thought of adaptation and assimilation is foreign to Israel, indeed, it is blasphemous. Israel's pariah existence in Egypt and its isolation in the desert seem permanently to have destroyed any sense of the possibility, and necessity, of self-assertion by means of political sagacity and civilizational behavior. Moreover, once the mechanism of this misunderstanding had been set in motion, each new disaster became an affirmation of a belief that had anticipated and even encouraged disaster in the first place. An unbroken chain of misfortune was a confirmation of the existence and the promise of Yahweh. Since the Jewish people expected deliverance to come from him, and not from themselves, none ever came. The end of it all was dispersion and flight out of history, with Christianity, meanwhile, arising along one of these routes of escape. And whether modern Judaism can make up in contemporary Israel for thousands of years of neglecting a sense of the actual and a readiness to adapt must remain in doubt, so long as the Jews do not, of their own volition, free themselves from the myth of deliverance through setting themselves apart.

Inseparable from the historical situation which molded Israel's belief is the landscape in the midst of which its destiny was consummated. This destiny reflects the rigors of the desert which throws men back upon themselves, for they have nothing to pit against its overpowering monotony but the strength of their imagination and intellect and the rigorous discipline of the community within which they feel secure. For the Israel of Biblical times the desert is not a living-space and home. Nor is it felt as nature, a place where God holds sway and makes himself known. It is a no-man's land, a boundary area between the one God and the one people. God is a personal and concrete, and not a mythical, deity. The human collectivity is the arena of synthesis for dialogue and argument with this deity. Thus the people themselves are again made the center and source of Jewish existence. Security and refuge lie only in strict adherence to the way of the community. On these terms alone is it possible to understand and tolerate the fact that God led his people out of the loneliness of slavery into the desert's loneliness. Moses does not bring dark, oracular pronouncements from Mount Sinai, but tables of law. On these tablets is clearly written down beyond any mistaking how Israel must live in order to be pleasing in Yahweh's sight and worthy of his promise. Thus the Jewish people developed not only a strongly defined consciousness of historical deliverance, but a powerful sense of a divinely decreed social order as well. There is nothing "worldly" in this theocracy. On the contrary, everything gets its meaning from God's command. A strict belief in the law arises—a pedantic, letter-perfect allegiance—which in turn leads to a concentration of all the formidable strength of the Jewish intelligence on the right interpretation of the Torah.

History and landscape have now fused, and have made of Israel a people of unexampled self-reference, exclusiveness and idiosyncrasy. In the face of the desert, the terrible lostness of the people who find themselves marooned as strangers in a world hostile to Judaism is a characteristic experience. The situation breeds an attitude whereby serious significance is attached to the world's emptiness and hostility. God is without form or face, and nature contains nothing worth knowing, expressing or delineating in its own right. No occasion exists for playful or probing pursuit of things outside the human sphere. Only that which proceeds out of God's unfettered will and man's spoken word has meaning and duration. These things represent and express an autonomous intellectuality. The desert's uniformity affords no occasion to test thought on objective processes and variations, or to seek after relationships independent of human speculation. Heat and cold, thunder and lightning, storm and flood are no more thought of as natural phenomena than slavery and persecution, need and denial are thought of as phenomena of an historical process. Both categories are conceived as evidencing God's masterful will, which demands humbleness and submission. This passionate readiness to accept suffering in apposition evokes the idealistic and wishful idea of a Promised Land, in which joy and fulfillment, the soft and brightly colored splendors of a paradise hold sway. But release from the fateful dominion of chosenness is not a possibility to be realized here and now. It is a promise shimmering far away in a distant future.

The peculiarity of the Jewish concept of the world begins to stand out clearly only when we see it against the background of other peoples' ways of life and religious ideas. In the tropic lands of southeast Asia, where men grow up amid a luxuriance of natural forms, a richness which Judaism projects into the distant time of deliverance, we find a diametrically opposed wish to flee from this riotous excess. The final goal in this case is not an idealized externalization of the conditions of life on earth, but release from the cycle of becoming and passing away. In east Asia, in polar opposition to the super-elevation of consciousness and the human personality, the reduction of history to theology and concrete adherence to the law, we find contempt for everything individual and everything pertaining to consciousness and history. To these people the world is God's confused dream, not the arena of his purposeful workings.

Only in the temperate zone do we find a balance between man

and the world around him. Here man is neither completely thrown back on himself, nor ensnared in a rampant waxing and waning of colors, forms and configurations from which he wishes nothing more than to escape. The distance between man and the world is neither too great to bridge nor so little that it becomes constrictive and suffocating. Man is able to gain enough clearance between himself and nature so as not to feel engulfed. Yet his apartness from nature is not so exaggerated that he becomes unaware of being bound up with it. He knows that he belongs to nature, and yet at the same time is apart from it. He senses that both he and the natural world belong to a great, inclusive system of relationships. Holding sway over the gods of both the Greeks and Romans and those of the Germanic tribes is a world-destiny and world-law to which gods and men are equally subject. While Judaism seeks to overcome the religion of many gods but meanwhile explains the essence of its one God in terms of his transcendence—his being apart from and above nature, his supernaturalness—European and many other peoples hold fast to their polytheistic ideas. But these gods of nature remain personifications of elemental powers and real phenomena close to humankind. Manifold links bind the worlds of gods and men. And that which is stronger than both gods and men is represented neither as a personal deity, nor as an other-worldly power above and opposed to the world. This godhead is rather in and of the world, a lawfulness at work everywhere.

This kind of understanding of the world and self, and the images and ideas by which it is apprehended, turn man's interest to the objective investigation of the phenomena of his environment. Man, in sum, is not completely encapsulated within himself. He experiences nature as something more than the expression and object of a divine will. Nature becomes to him an object of cognition, something out there to be looked into. Out of a mythology of nature a philosophy of nature develops, and, in turn, scientific thought. Among the Greeks of the pre-Socratic period, as early as c. 600 B.C., suddenly appear all the considerations and motives later taken up by European philosophy and science: an attempt to trace back all phenomena to an ultimate substance (such as water or fire) or to a final principle derivative from nature (becoming or being); and the discovery of objective laws governing nature which make it possible to see into and make use of natural processes. In the same centuries Indian thinkers of the Vedic period tried to deduce the meaning of life from observation of nature. But their deliberations unfolded entirely in the realm of philosophical and religious speculation. Here Indian thought is interested in the investigation of nature only to the extent that this search throws light on the intrinsic character, the essence of the world, thus showing mankind how to extricate itself from its entanglement. The exploration of nature pursued for its own sake, and in order to master and utilize natural powers, is completely alien to this kind of thinking. However, we must not lose sight of the fact that in this general endeavor the ancient Indian thinkers were the first "incidentally" to develop the foundations of mathematics, astronomy and medicine.

The point where Indian and Greek thinking parted company can be very clearly shown. It occurred upon encountering the theme of metempsychosis, or the transmigration of souls. In both Greece and India the contemplation of nature led to the discovery of life's universally cyclical character. From this thinkers of both cultures concluded that human beings are repeatedly born anew. But whereas in Greece the belief in reincarnation achieved only transitory significance and was soon shelved, in India it became a basic idea penetrating all philosophical and religious systems throughout thousands of years, even to the present time. In short, an inevitable consequence of the idea of the transmigration of souls was

to bolster the need to think of man's salvation in terms of deliverance from the eternal cycle of becoming and passing away. Whatever might enhance the possibility of release from the endless
chain of rebirth then spontaneously became thought of as "doing
the right thing." In Greek thought, quite to the contrary, the
concept of the cyclical became fundamental to the idea of causality,
and so eventually became the basis of a scientific approach to the
world.

The Germanic peoples were never able to take the step from
myth to natural philosophy, since Christian monotheism supplanted their original polytheism. Their rediscovery of the philosophies of antiquity and, by this roundabout route, of their own
philosophical mode and gift, came relatively late. The western
and northern European peoples' distorted relationship with their
past can be traced back to this powerful Christian subvention.
Since the Germanic people view their own pre-Christian past as
a sort of barbarian dawn of history, every Germanist philosophy
develops a tendency toward conscious reversion to the barbaric,
while every anti-Germanist philosophy is deeply tinged with resentment that a primitive barbarism should be identified with
the fundamental German nature. Among all these peoples the
phase corresponding to the one in which the Germans were civilized
by Christianity is deemed barbaric. One of the deepest and most
hidden sources of northern peoples' anti-Christian feeling is certainly rooted in the shock of violent conversion, the feeling of
having had one's own natural development betrayed.

Jewish thought, meanwhile, as it develops becomes completely
alienated from nature. No objective experience figures in its picture
of the world. The nature-god, Yahweh, becomes the god of
history.

Originally Yahweh was the personification of some natural force, probably volcanism. But this original personification was more or less done away with, not in such fashion, however, that its constituent natural elements came into view, but rather so as to empty it entirely of objective content and make it into a principle sufficient unto itself. In other words, the anthropomorphic personality which had been read into nature was not canceled out, but released from nature and elevated to the highest spiritual rank. The bond between man and nature was severed. In this concept God is an abstraction, devoid of all actualness, and insulated from human understanding of whatever kind or degree. God becomes an ego raised above all dimension. Since the key attribute of human personality is free will, free will becomes God's most distinctive attribute. His existence and greatness are evidenced by the circumstance that he makes himself known to mankind in acts without any motive except to exemplify the divine will. The personal god must be an incomprehensible god, a god who does not reward those who obey his commands, or punish them because he has been injured. It is out of his own inscrutable might and fullness of authority that he damns or blesses. Ultimate obedience is shown him by the humble acceptance of anything that he may ordain. He is the complete otherness, the absolutely free will, the autonomous superego, standing in opposition to the world that he has created.

The process of refinement whereby the wrathful and violent tribal god of the Jews is transformed into the mild patriarch and father of Christianity actually does not alter this deity's essential nature. He is and remains a daemon, a supernatural force residing outside the world's context, a deity whose impenetrable decisions constantly remind man of his nothingness. But since peoples do not devise their religions in order to confirm their impotence, but to escape their weakness and misery, a possibility of communication has to be invented between the inexplicable ruler-god and his chosen people. Thus was God attributed with the will occasionally to manifest himself, for reasons unknown and under arcane circumstances, to certain single, select people. The boon of divine manifestation is a kind of bridge thrown out by God to connect this world and regions of divinity. This form of communication, however, is by no means the result of any human effort. It is a purely arbitrary concession. Man cannot come near to God either through deed or through insight. But whoever happens to be chosen by God as mediator becomes excellent above all others. It is he who announces and protects the law, and only through his intervention can eternal damnation be escaped. In this concessive acceptance by God is grounded the prophets' significance and the dominant position of the priests and scholars who interpret the texts and ensure ritual observance.

The writings of the Old Testament are regarded as God's immediate dictates and utterances. The word is magic. Whoever possesses it and knows how to use it properly has power over men and things. Indeed, anyone able to express his own human will and knowledge by means of signs and letters must to some degree be a medium of divine power, or even God's mouthpiece. When Moses brings the tablets of the law to the Jews, it is not necessary for him expressly to say that they have been dictated by God. It simply could not have been otherwise. The Jewish people have always had a special attachment to the word. The power of clearly formulated thinking and writing transformed simple tribal herdsmen and agriculturalists into an historically conscious folk. The word exists by virtue of an act of intellection. Conceptual abstraction lifts it above myth. Here and now and thus, and in no other way, are to be fulfilled the things for which Israel was divinely chosen. In sum, God expresses himself with precision. He is a capricious deity, but also an exact one, who loves concreteness and clarity.

Two basic characteristics of Christianity are allied to these elements of Jewish belief. One is the idea of an autonomous, personal god resident in the beyond, yet at work in the world of the living. The other is the conviction that this deity has unequivocally laid down for all peoples and all time his will's intent by the prosecution of certain events and writings. Judaism and Christianity represent the perpetuation, in effect, of a primitive theology. The road to philosophy and science is barred. Any acceptance of the idea that nature and history follow their own laws would have ascribed a certain degree of impotence to God, and to this extent would have been a denial of his willful and personal existence. Therefore, the solution of problems spontaneously arising from the human capacity to perceive objective relationships and to draw general conclusions therefrom could not take the form of a free investigation of things. Rather, it had to be confined to an interpretation of the textually embalmed expressions of God's will.

The Jews have produced visionaries and lawgivers, prophets and learned men, but never a Thales nor a Parmenides, a Plato or an Aristotle. It is not until Judaism comes into contact with Hellenistic culture, thus emancipating Jewish intellectuals from the purely Mosaic belief, that Jewish thinking in philosophy and science, made sharp, pliant and subtle by centuries of casuistry, begins to bear fruit. So extraordinary is the intellection of thinkers generated out of Judaism that the history of Western civilization would be unthinkable without their contribution. Modernity, in which the real epoch of the rational begins, owes a great deal of its motive power and revolutionary innovations to the towering accomplishments of Jewish scholars and scientists. But these isolated feats by Jews who have become emancipated from the orthodox

Judaic tradition and assimilated into the non-Jewish world actually represent only the obverse side of the fact that orthodox Jewry has remained stuck fast in a purely speculative and scholastic intellectualism, a kind of thinking which Christianity has taken over and played off against scientific thought since the days of the Apostle Paul. This sort of intellection consists of the ability, deemed higher than mere reason, to build up conceptual structures to dizzy heights out of whatever thesis may lie at hand.

Here, too, is one of the roots of that unhealthy dichotomy between the study of nature and the study of mind and spirit, a split that has left its mark on the whole mode of behavior and intellectual tradition of the West. This dichotomy has given rise to the circumstance that all that is subsumed in the Western World under the name of the "humanities" has developed an extravagant and empty idealism, an idealism which today as in other years deems it quite unnecessary—indeed, pedestrian—to control freewheeling speculation through experience and experiment.

A theologian is a man who never questions God, but talks about him as though divinity were an irreversible truth. He is a person who takes his stand on a certain answer before his searchings, and the answers to them, have actually reached the limit of his power to question and find answers. This leaves him with a residue of unused intellectual energy, which he is free to expend on the artistic elaboration of his theses, developing ideas to ripeness as he sees fit and discarding those he thinks false.

Christianity, however, is not simply a Jewish sect. Into it has emptied a second mighty river of religious thought. Only when both elements, the Jewish and the non-Jewish, have intermingled and modified each other do we have what is known as Christianity. The second stratum overlying the basic Jewish belief contains the religious ideas of various neighboring ancient peoples—the Assyrians, Babylonians, Persians and finally the Greeks. Christianity has borrowed from all of these. But in the last analysis Christianity still derives at bottommost level from Judaism. Its non-Jewish elements are adaptations added to the basic form. Since Biblical research began during the 18th-century Age of Enlightenment, there has always been a vague idea of the events which led to this development and the course it ran. But meanwhile, during later centuries, our knowledge of history, archeology, theology, philology, sociology and anthropology has increased so much that it is time to write a new and comprehensive history of the rise of Christianity. A new, if still not definitive, explanation of Christianity's immediate prehistory is seemingly afforded by the scrolls found in great numbers since 1947 on the western shore of the Dead Sea. These Dead Sea scrolls, written in Hebrew, stem from the Jewish religious community of Qumran, from which it has been inferred that they are directly connected with the Essene sect. The story of the discovery and evaluation of the Dead Sea scrolls reads like an exciting novel. It can be readily understood that both the Christian church and orthodox Jewry should greet the find with very mixed feelings. For whatever the scrolls may turn out to be, they indicate that Christianity did, at any rate, have a definite prehistory and did evolve out of the Jewish religion in a continuous series of political, social and ideological stages. Under such circumstances it is not easy to maintain the belief that Christ's teachings and all that appears in the Gospel could have been a sudden and unqualified revelation of the Son of God.

If the accumulated research of previous years is put together with this most recent information, the following picture takes shape. In the second century before Christ, a Jewish sect of reformist nature arose in Palestine. This sect, however, remained within the body of Judaism and along with the Sadducees and the Pharisees was true to the law. The remarkable thing about this sect was what might be called its political resignation. It gave up one of the essential ideas of the Mosaic belief, namely, an expectation of deliverance linked to the historical consolidation of Israel. Among this sect the Jewish people's helplessness and suffering cease to be signs of election. An individual readiness to suffer replaces the collective readiness. The individual becomes the object of divine ordeal and manifestation of divine bounty and chosenness. The mode of relationship with God is retained, but it now applies to the individual Jew, rather than to Jewry as a whole. At the same time the bestowal of God's favor continues to be more certain the more humiliated, persecuted, weak and needy one is.

The Essenes, however, go beyond adherence to traditional rules and regulations and traditional speculation. Their repudiation of the historico-political expectation of deliverance has a decisive consequence. They flee from the world and evolve into a monkish, ascetic order. Members of the sect dedicate their lives to God. But this vocation is no longer understood as living under the law within the Jewish community. It is a form of existence divorced from all social ties, a preparation for encounter with God carried out under strict regimentation and the maintenance of rules peculiar to the sect and a step beyond Judaism. These rules, which among the Essenes appear for the first time as ritual, include: baptism, meals of holy communion, sacred lustrations and vows of chastity, abstinence and seclusion.

This monastic idea of the Essenes, which was alien to Mosaic Judaism, and their equally alien cultistic practices, indicates that mere reformulation of existing Jewish religious belief was not enough for them. This would have been the case if, for example, they had contented themselves with making a personal-existential idea of deliverance out of the historico-collective model. But their negative turning aside from the orthodox tradition also involved giving it a new and positive content taken from foreign religions. Their main source of innovation is the Persian doctrine of the two worlds, the Kingdom of Light and the Kingdom of Darkness. On Judgment Day—an idea, incidentally, found nowhere in the Mosaic religion—the Messiah will pronounce judgment, rewarding the good and delivering the wicked over to eternal pain. Earthly existence is a prelude to the joys of the hereafter. Also peculiar to the creed of the people of Qumran, at least in the early stage of their development, appears to be a feeling of pugnacious anger toward the wicked. However, the most significant result of the new teaching is a radical division of souls here and now, in this world, into the good and bad.

Whereas Jewish dualism was exclusively metaphysical, with a supernatural God standing opposed to his creation, in the dualism which now developed creation itself is split asunder, with one segment consigned to eternal damnation, the other to eternal blessedness. A conviction basic to the Jewish religion is the idea that not only is everything in the world created by God, but this entirety, being of divine origin, must be good. But for the Qumran sect and the Essenes there is a light and a dark side to the world, aspects corresponding to heaven and hell in the hereafter. Not only individuals but whole peoples are either damned or blessed. This outlook contains more than the belief in election exclusively for the suffering and oppressed. It also expresses a need, cloaked in religion, for quittance and revenge on those who have caused the suffering and oppression. Resentment creeps into the hitherto inviolate conception of the Mosaic faith, a disputatious attribution of devilishness to unbelievers and outsiders. The Jews leave to God's inscrutable providence the question of how other peoples will fare in this world and in the hereafter. The Essenes believe they can anticipate his decision on this score. And since they know beforehand, it must therefore be pleasing in God's sight if they reinforce his retributive judgment by taking up arms against the children of darkness and their machinations.

In sum, man is expected to take partisan action against God's enemies. The anthropological dualism of the body vs. the soul imprisoned in it which would have rounded out the precedent moral dualism does not, however, appear among the Essenes. This dualism does not evolve in full trenchancy until Manichaeism and Platonism are incorporated into Christianity, though even then without complete success. For the Christian belief in "the resurrection of the body" shows that the Old Testament comment on creation—"and behold, it was good"—remains fundamental in Christian as well as in Judaic dogma. At the same time anthropological dualism in connection with the concepts of sin and original sin have played an important role in the Christian ethic and the psychology of Christian peoples.

In the ritual of the Qumran order, alongside the doctrine of two worlds, appears a strong magical element, probably derivative from Babylonian-Assyrian sources. This element consists of a belief that certain actions bring one closer to God, indeed, into unity with him. A life pleasing to God is no longer dependent on the observance of the customs and rites of the law, but rather on participation in mystic acts, which must be fulfilled in a cult-community cut off from the rest of the world. How to go about performing these rites is esoteric knowledge, a cabalistic body of teaching. Mainstays of the Essene cult are sacred lustrations or washings and holy feasts of communion. Basic to them is the idea that a divine power resides in certain elemental things, such as water, and that this healing property can be shared by those who know how to use it in the right way.

In this case the acceptance of the idea that something can be conjured forth by magic is bound up with old beliefs stemming from the vegetation mysteries. According to these mysteries, participation in the waning and waxing of the seasons—whereby the acts of dying and resurrection are symbolically accomplished—ensures union with the divine, rebirth and eternal life. These sacred nature rites, as known among the Essenes, are not, however, a form of true nature magic, of coercion, as it were, directed toward God by those in possession of the mystery. On the contrary, they are practiced on an unshakably monotheistic basis. These rites are paths to deliverance ordained by God for the use of those who seek him. The bridge to redemption still remains a benefit proceeding from God's side of the chasm, not from man's. Thus magic loses the character of a device which man, out of his own strength and knowledge, can use for deliverance.

It is important to get this Essene point of view clearly in mind, for it shows how completely a theocratic world-concept, once rigidly laid down, blocks off every avenue to philosophical thinking and a natural "religion." Both magical thinking and the mythical cosmology of the old mystery-religions by progressive conceptual refinement came to develop intuitive forms consonant with reality. Magic is the precursor of causationism, the first intimation that all things are interconnected and that influence over them can be gained if one knows their mode of relationship, and how to take advantage of it. And the vegetation mysteries are an early assurance of the fact that man belongs within the natural scheme, that natural processes repeat themselves in him, and his history within their midst. This possibility of arriving at a correct understanding of the world by a continuous intellectual development out of magic and myth exists because in both instances, magic and myth, the point of departure and the speculative material are concerned with nature, and with the structural laws and factual content of natural phenomena.

But the opportunity of spiritual escape offered by the adoption of Babylonian-Assyrian rites slipped through the Essenes' fingers. They remained trapped in their theocentric cul-de-sac. They emptied their appropriated magic-mystic practices of naturalistic content and made them over into rites arbitrarily laid down by God. The evolution of magical and mystical modes of viewing into the Christian sacraments, and into the other manifold sacred acts of a theologized magic, such as the veneration of relics, was accomplished among the Essenes during the last two centuries before Christ. What had been the interpretation of being generated by a naïve, yet nonetheless realistic mode of thought was made into the world-picture of a speculative and absurdity-seeking theosophy. The theocentric and rationalistic set of Jewish beliefs spoiled all elements drawn from nature-religion during the metamorphosis into Christianity. These elements became arid abstractions, devoid of factuality and sense, completely divorced from the natural background whence they had sprung.

For example, in all vegetation cults, sexual congress is conceived as a mystery, in which the ecstasy of the procreative act and the act itself are intended to be understood as a symbol of cosmic powers at work everywhere throughout nature. But when Christianity decides to release man from nature's toils, the mystery of Eros becomes the ruttish scandal of sex, a phenomenon so offensive that not even the sacrament of marriage purifies it, but rather actualizes it and makes it visible. The banishment and perversion of the procreative into the merely sexual, with all its consequent psychic and moral ravages, is the completely typical decomposition product of a nature-hating spiritualism. Whoever has studied the relevant modes of thought and behavior of non-

Christian cultures needs neither Friedrich Nietzsche nor Sigmund Freud to convince himself of the truth of this statement.

Judaism was alienated from the world, but not life-hating. This attitude, by a process of rigorous suppression, was initiated by Christianity. Its course can be traced in the official acts of the early Christian councils, which made the nature-religion origins of Christian magic unrecognizable. It is on this account that it is erroneous to connect Jewish-Christian religiosity with the concept of myth. The Jewish creed—in contrast to nearly all Indo-Germanic ideas of the cosmos—was an historical metaphysic, and as such not a nature mythos but a religious ideology. And those elements of Christianity which originated in myth were uprooted and ossified into abstract miracles.

The Christian transformation of the Jewish belief in a messiah is also connected with the absorption of magic-mystic ideas via the Essenes. In Old Testament times a messiah was an anointed high priest. Later, in expectation of the coming kingdom of fulfillment, the messiah became the future king of the Jews, ruler of salvation's realm. But it was far from Jewish monotheism to conceive this messiah as an embodiment of God. Among the Essenes, however, this same concrete historico-political anticipation, which tied in the messiah idea with Judaism, suffered a transformation, in keeping with their hostile attitude toward history. With them the anointed messiah becomes God's agent, a leader of the children of light in their war against the children of darkness. A prophet of the Essene sect, the so-called "teacher of uprightness," an historical personage of the century before Christ, appears to have been regarded as this kind of messiah. The documents of the people of Qumran indicate that they were written under the direct influence of this messiah's prophecies. Many of the late Jewish apocryphal and apocalyptic writings also arose in this same atmosphere.

The significance of the teacher of uprightness is a much debated question, but he undoubtedly anticipated Christ's role. He is God's suffering servant, prophet and martyr, harbinger and sacrificial victim of his faith, and high judge on Judgment Day. The themes of his sacrificial death and his heavenly judgmental function beyond question pave the way for the Christian version of the belief in a messiah. The messiah is made into divine manifestation. However, myths common to many religions of a god-man who sacrifices himself to save the world and of a light-god who hands down judgment —this last concept borrowed from the Parsic (Zoroastrian) religion —could be incorporated into a dualistic theology only by transposing the attributes and functions invested in the messiah in question to God's side of the dualistic picture. The idea that human self-sacrifice might have deliverance potential, or that a man could sit at God's side in judgment, would have been intolerable to the Jewish spirit, permeated as it was by the conviction that man was all creature-like. The eternal becoming and passing away of nature, the mysterious intermeshment of which in mythical thinking is exemplified in the image of a god sacrificed only to rise again, in Christianity becomes an unnatural miracle of bodily resurrection and a unique, never-to-be-repeated historical event. Out of the need to imprison a continuing, pervasive natural phenomenon in an image and a fable, an attempt was made against all reason to rationalize the myth and to attach it exclusively to the life and death of Christ as an historical person.

Just as the tie-in between Israelite history and Israelite belief in God determined the uniqueness of Judaism, similarly Christianity's claim of exclusiveness rests on a belief in a once-occurring disclosure of self by God in Christ. For the Christian metaphysic is also a limited, historical metaphysic. In this case, however, what among the Jews was understood as one particular people's sacred history was elevated into the sacred history of all mankind. The promise of redemption in and through history, meanwhile, was transposed into the hereafter. In this frame of reference the history of mankind, to whom God has declared himself and summoned to redemption, is really history, since it has a fixed beginning and an irrevocable end in time. St. Paul and the church fathers theologically formulated and dogmatized this theory.

Islam has preserved the character of a strict monotheism, since Mohammed was only the prophet and founder of the new faith. As for Buddha, he never claimed to be anything but a man, differing from other men only in his deeper insight. All that distinguished Buddha from any ordinary philosopher was the fact that he did not so much strive to acquire and teach knowledge of the world as to show men a way whereby they could break their way out of the world's cyclical confines. All he asked of others was that they give his avenue of deliverance a personal trial. He laid down no qualifications in point of belief in his person, or in any kind of metaphysical postulate. Actually Christ is the only founder of a religion who conceived himself to be the incarnation of the divine will and essence, and who viewed himself as a personal engine of salvation. To be sure, Christ also expected great moral effort from those who hoped to win God's grace, but this effort is not the supplicant's decisive commitment. The key is belief in Christ, in his divine kinship and divine intercession.

Having made it our thesis that Christ was prefigured, or at any rate strongly influenced, by the Jewish reform movement of the Essenes, we can also spell out what distinguishes Christ from them. Whereas the founding of the Essenic order was a spontaneous turning away from the world of the senses to a cenobite and ascetic religiosity, Christ led his believers back into the world. Not back, it must be borne in mind, into any religious community, but simply back among men, into life as it is commonly lived. In other words, the Christian repudiation of the Judaic historico-political form of deliverance did not, as the Essenes' similar repudiation did, give rise to retrogression. Rather, it neutralized the political consideration, while at the same time it gave it a religious tone. God shall be given what is his, Caesar what is his. When religious solicitation was narrowed down to belief in Christ, the Essenes' cenobitic ideals lost their meaning. Self-immurement from the world is not the thing, but individual power of belief. And this power can be unfolded and evidenced in the world precisely because in the world the believer is exposed to constant humiliation and persecution, that is, to undeserved suffering, which makes him pleasing in God's sight and accessible to God's reality and truth. This doctrine prepares Christianity for emergence both from Judaism and sectarianism. No longer is it bound to a particular people or an exclusive way of life. It can be lived and experienced by anyone willing to believe.

A new ethic now arises in accordance with this return to the world. Christ leaves the Jewish creed behind. True, he also commands obedience to the law. But he strives to get beyond the law, too, for real salvation no longer lies in its interpretation and fulfill-ment. As for the Essenes' ascetic ethic, it is useless for living in the world, even though its trace is indelibly impressed on Christian memory. Christ preaches an enthusiastic, idealistic ethic, a summons to love mankind, not so much opposed to the world's way as blind to it and wishful of overcoming it. It is characterized by a readiness, even a desire, to suffer, and by limitless compassion for all who are poor and oppressed. From the Nazarene must have radiated a fascination in the face of which a mere striving for justice must have seemed impotent and small. The Jewish people understood suffering as a test but were far from inclined to love those who made them suffer. The Jewish religious way conquered suffering by absorbing fate's buffets into the Jewish will. Christ not only makes suffering a mark of distinction, but even envelops the authors of suffering into his will, thus rendering them defenseless. It is this world-encompassing message of love which makes Christianity's whole motivation an event that goes beyond the historical, sociological or psychological, which indeed marks one of the peaks of human history, to the extent that it is a history of ethical ideals.

From the standpoint of religious history, relative to Judaism Christianity was, in a sense, an involutional event, a going back toward more primitive intuitions. Its borrowings from the Persians, Babylonians and Assyrians were a barbarization of Jewish monotheism. Its superiority depends solely on its message of love and its willingness to love. It is these qualities which ensured its victory over Judaism as well as over an intellectually superior Hellenistic philosophy. It was a message that turned people away from their earthly misery toward deliverance, and not toward the elite and the elite's pursuit of knowledge. The power and splendor of these joyous tidings, however, should not be allowed to gloss over the fact that it was a utopian ethic that they heralded, a morality that set the human heart on fire, but found no purchase in human nature. It was an idealistic morality, which taxed mankind beyond its capacity, and therefore failed by a wide margin to live up to its claim of being the one given point of departure from which man can be bettered in and for the world. Thus, in the history of the Western World arose a characteristic conflict between an extreme sensitization of the conscience and an equally striking inability among Christians to lead a "truly Christian" life.

The Christian message of love, moreover, could be made understandable and convincing only to the extent that it succeeded in modifying the harsh Judaic notion of man as God's passive instrument and the Essenic teaching of predestination toward good or evil. This was accomplished by developing the theory of forgiveness through Christ and, by proxy, through the church. It also proved possible to amalgamate the idea of forgiveness of sin through Christ and his deputies with the idea of God's free will, by conceiving man's capacity to believe as a sign of divine sympathy. The why of it, the reason for God's grace, remained far beyond human understanding. But henceforth the possibility existed of ascertaining when this boon had been granted, and who had been chosen to receive it. The ability to believe in Christ as messiah indicated that God was favorably inclined toward the believer and agreeable to the forgiveness of his sins. "He that believeth in Christ is born again!" The experience of belief as here posited is quite different from the Judaic form of belief. The Judaic form consists in zealous adherence to the revealed law; the Christian form in ecstatic surrender to a personality. The Christian experience of faith is an act of unconditional and passionate self-renunciation, in which the catharsis of the vegetation cult reappears. In these cults intoxication, dancing and sexual excitement were the means used to evoke rapture and a spilling out of feeling, intended to bring about a fusion of man and the godhead. The drama of Christian divine love eschewed such Dionysiac practices and sensations. The Christian act of uniting oneself with God the son and God the father is now entirely understood and emphasized as an occurrence within the soul. Nevertheless, in its psychological structure it is still a spiritualized form of the heathen orgy. What happens is a sudden splitting asunder and inversion of human nature.

Under these conditions the state of "unbelievingness" of many men is bound to seem virtually unalterable. Actually, however, the true Christian way to faith depends on a drastic reorganization of the inner self, though the resulting enrichment is very much open to question. But this consideration does not strike at the heart of the matter. The real point is, catharsis occurs only if God so desires and wills. If Christians took this conviction seriously, church pews would never be filled with believers. But even if it is admitted that the nature and intensity of the experience of faith under some circumstances cannot be completely understood by the believer himself, let alone by an outsider, the question of relating "believers"—including supposititious ones—and "unbelievers" still should be susceptible to an answer. It is surely needful of one. The definitive part played by God's approval in the experience of belief must necessarily prevent any Christian from looking on the "belieflessness" of the "unbelievers" as grounded in their evil will. Indeed, it is precisely among Christians that we have a right to expect understanding of the fact that a man who is denied the ability to believe in God nonetheless must go on living as best he can and in so doing fashion a view of the world in keeping with his lack of "enlightenment." One of the many inconsequences of Christianity, whose founder was a genius of loving understanding, is that the churches and their adherents only rarely are inclined to provide this kind of understanding.

4

THE PSYCHOLOGICAL GROUNDS
FOR EUROPE'S CONVERSION

THE CHRISTIAN CULTURE of the West arose in a field of stress lying between a general outlook characterized by an affinity for the objective world and by an affirmative seeking to discover the unity and order of being and an opposed outlook marked by hostility toward nature and a tendency toward dualism and the speculative. To the extent that this culture was Christian or, more accurately, Catholic, we must view humanism and the Reformation not only as defections from the "true doctrine of Christ," but as defections from the "West" as well. As we look back on the Western World as what it was and later became outside Christianity, that is, apart from any relation to Christian religiosity, on the whole it can be best defined for our purposes as "Western," "Continental" or "European." This European or Continental quality may be thought of as referring to all those genuinely indigenous tendencies which—at first overlaid and suppressed by Christianity

—gradually reappeared, and which in our times can be conceptually separated from the specifically Christian mode of feeling
and picturing the world. The tremendous intellectual and psychic
tension which of necessity arose in the attempt to marry two such
disparate kinds of thinking, found expression not only in ingenious
religious, philosophical, esthetic, moral and political theories, but
in the literary and artistic monuments of the golden age of the
Christian West.

But in marveling at these cultural achievements we must not
lose sight of the fact that the Christianization of the Continental
peoples was by no means an event foreordained since Adam's day.
On the contrary it was a matter of chance, just as it is typical of
human experience to be born by "chance" into this or that set
of social circumstances, an environmental set which seems completely natural to the one born to it. In this connection it might
be asked whether a European development without Christian
influence would not have been weak and colorless. To this question
there is no conclusive answer. But who would care to dispute the
hypothesis that a Buddhistic Europe very likely would also have
achieved great things in all fields of art and science? Actually, the
passive, environmentally determined characteristics of Buddhism
would have been much more easily Europeanized than was Christianity. For Christianity, though very activist, did not accord with
the reality of nature and humankind. Moreover, Christianity went
against the Continental peoples' understanding of the world,
whereas the Buddhistic attitude merely ran counter to their
temperament.

In any event, there can be no doubt that had European thinking
been allowed to develop undisturbed, it would have led to a very
much different world-construct than the one offered by the
Christian metaphysic. All peoples whose history runs its course

under relatively favorable climatic and political conditions, sooner or later arrive at some sort of universalist and dynamic outlook on the cosmos. So far as it is possible to find a common denominator among the multiplicity of viewpoints generated by these unfettered peoples, they develop—in whatever situation they are in a position to master—an attitude toward life focused around man as a being who probes into, reacts and accords recognition to, and impresses order on, the surrounding world. The day comes when what were originally thought of as gods or spirits are recognized as natural phenomena and as such given a place within the great net of natural events. The world's mystery crystallizes into a prime cause of all being, conceived now as person, now as primeval energy. A pantheistic notion of the world spontaneously evolves from a daemonistic-materialistic polytheism. From this an immanence or identity metaphysic eventually develops. The idea of something "divine" at work in all human beings and all things leads to the ontological identification of being and existence, under whichever of their various aspects "being" and "existence" may be regarded.

Characteristic of this type of ideology is its disposition, familiar to all of us of the West, to think in terms of facts and events experienced objectively by man, in complete independence of his individual dreams and collective visions. Also typical is the value assigned the power of human reason to confront the data of experience without bias. "Without bias" naturally does not mean that the individual can hoist himself by his bootstraps and rid himself entirely of the ideological and psychological limitations of his particular level of consciousness. It simply means that he is able to portray reality, in idea and language, in a structurally correct fashion. This object-directed understanding of the world makes possible the emergence of scientific investigation and control of the world. All our accumulation of scientific experience and for-

mulation, as a matter of fact, can be fitted not only into the
Greco-Roman picture of the world, but even into the basic sche-
mata of the great Indian philosophical systems, even though the
advancement of technology and the sciences holds no interest for
them. From the Copernican to the Einsteinian cosmogony to the
new genetic and depth psychologies there is nothing that cannot
be harmonized with these ancient peoples' religious ideas. All
empiric and discursive (analytic) cognition consists of particulars
which can be assigned a place, after the fact, in a general image
that has been correctly visualized in the first place and to begin
with interpreted as a wholeness. In Thales, first of the Greek
philosophers, we find a conviction that all things have developed
from a common source. In the fifth century before Christ, Buddha
came forward with a way to release through meditation based on
a highly differentiated psychology, according to which the soul
is not a state, but a process. And even the Germanic religion, as
barbarous as it was and as bare of any real philosophical spirit,
under the coarse mantle of its epics of gods and heroes shows an
unmistakable sense of the interwovenness of all things.

Compared with the foregoing, Christianity is the prototype of the
antiphilosophic and antiscientific outlook on the world. This
essential inclination, which goes back to the Jewish religion, for
many years enhanced rather than hindered the spread of Christianity. The masses of the ancient and medieval world were quite
unable to judge the truth-value of a religious world-image. They
needed a form of teaching able to touch their hearts directly, in
the very midst of their human afflictions. This is exactly what
Christianity did. Its message of deliverance "through belief alone"
gave promise of life lived in fulfillment and truth to precisely those
people who lacked worldly possessions and knowledge, and who,
on account of their social origin and position, could not even

hope ever to share in the knowledge and accomplishments of their times. This depressed class of humanity spontaneously generated its own representation and leadership, men who were educated enough clearly to feel dissatisfied with their situation, yet not perceptive enough to see that improving their lot was a political task. Thus, their criticisms were directed not so much against existing conventions as against the drift and meaning of the social order. All the criteria developed by antiquity fell into disuse, for sheer lack of anyone with the ability to make use of them. A need meanwhile had arisen which permitted what passed as truth to be gained at one swoop, by taking a short cut around the traditional road. The burning impatience of those condemned to ignorance allowed no scope for anything but the idea of salvation, the apprehension of which required nothing except its simple avowal.

It is of the essence in any religion to make the promise of redemption independent of all social and intellectual accomplishment, and to predicate its consummation exclusively on an inward individual preparedness. However, when we bear in mind the fact that in Buddhism fulfillment comes only as the fruit of unexampled moral, psychic and intellectual self-discipline, and that both Judaism and Islam call for the observance of rigorous social and ritualistic prescripts, it becomes clear that Christianity is the extreme instance of a religion founded purely on belief. So dominant is the idea that Christians are made elect of God by unconditional surrender to Christ that the significance of moral effort and loyalty to the law pales beside it, and any intellectual striving to reach the truth seems absurd and even dangerous. Although Paul came into very close contact with the philosophies of his time, and in his epistles shows that he was particularly influenced by the Stoics, he still considers philosophical knowledge not only of trivial value, but the whole enterprise basically pointless and productive of error. He turned not only against his own people's idea of justification through God's workings, but also against the then-ruling Stoic and Epicurean philosophies. In the joyous message delivered by his Lord, Jesus Christ, he saw a way to salvation which not only made its believers equal to all Jews and pagans, but in addition gave them a dignity and a kind of knowledge never to be attained through learning or faithfulness to the law. The feeling of humility in the obverse was a feeling of superiority. Christians ceased to envy anyone. On the contrary, they pitied all those who clung to the mistaken view that a man must exercise his own strength and will to pass muster before God and men.

Every religion and ideology has its sociological aspects, and the fact that a certain social situation favors the propagation of a religion or ideology is no guarantee of its intrinsic truth. Moreover, we are forced to suspect that in the case of a concept of salvation so clearly designed to provide social compensation, its triumphal progress depended less on the persuasiveness of its argument than on the needs generated by social stress. The aristocrat and the middle-class person are able to produce more fruitful ideas than the serf, the smallholder, and the lower-middle-class person because they are more secure and not because they are innately superior in point of intelligence. Buddha was the son of a Nepalese prince and Buddhism was disseminated and made a success by the ruling Aryan warrior caste. It was precisely on account of this aristocratic background that Buddha appealed to man's self-confidence and self-awareness, rather than to his fears and doubts. The sage living in terms of his own inner security and the fullness of his own intellectual strength, who forsakes the world out of an awareness of superiority, or the self-possessed philosopher who calmly devotes his life to studying the way of the world, are prototypes who do not figure in the purview of people attracted by Christianity. The Christian, as it were, wishes the redeemer, prophet and saint into existence, all these in one, and this one makes no demands on his adherent's will to help himself, but promises salvation as a gift. The world is not to be overcome, but conquered by abrogation. The Jews as a people were permanently trapped in a situation from which there was no escape, yet as individuals they found security and dignity in their firmly fashioned tribal structure. The Christian likewise found a footing only in his own religious community, and likewise derived self-confidence therefrom. But this worked only so long and so far as he was prepared to cut all ties with his people and his social station, and to renounce all consciousness of his own worth.

This ideology of self-renunciation, of belief in surrendering to a redeemer and in the unconditional avowal of the idea of salvation proclaimed by him as imbued with redemptive power—an ideology of this sort comes into being only when a society has deprived large groups among its membership of this world's goods and of all prospect of remedying the lack. To the extent that history is a "class struggle"—although naturally it is much more than this—this state of affairs is obviously characteristic of any revolutionary movement. The history of European utopianism and sectarianism also shows the close relation between social degradation and belief in miracles. This holds for political as well as mystical theories of redemption, since belief in the power of black and white magic is nothing more or less than a form of compensation for those who are impatient to see their paradise on earth quickly realized through destruction of the existing order. The real root of all hope in a sudden, drastic revolution transforming all things is always the feeling that individual man, dependent on himself alone, is impotent and lost, and can be saved only by the miraculous.

Nothing less than a new social order, at once peaceful and mobile, can neutralize this fateful mechanism, a scheme of things in which not only are need and misery suppressed, but beyond which every man has an equal chance to win possessions, status and education.

But it is the concept of the democratic state which first makes it possible for members of all classes to develop that minimum trust in one's own strength that in turn holds in check the hope of salvation through a miracle. In Western countries the Communist Manifesto was balked not by any counterideology, but by the circumstance that we are living in a period of general well-being and universal opportunity for every man to better himself. And the "incapacity to believe" and "reluctance to believe" so long deplored by the church, is a result of the fact, among other things, that the climate of a democratic and individualistic way of life premises a will to self-help and self-release hard to reconcile with a redemptive power possessed exclusively by supernatural and superhuman beings. This is a conflict, incidentally, that cannot arise in Buddhism. All Buddhists can somehow, sometime conceivably become a Buddha. But no Christian can ever become a Christ. In Christianity the authoritarian-patriarchal relation of the believers to the founder of their religion has been made completely absolute and eternal. No amount of human striving can alter this fact. From this point of view, then, Buddhism is a democratic type of religion, Christianity an autocratic type.

Although Christianity was a movement directly produced by the social chaos of antiquity, its founder did not intend it to have political consequences, nor did his creed contain this possibility. The historical forces which generated Christianity and set it in motion simply came to be assimilated willy-nilly into the pattern of religious expectation. The first great revolt of oppressed and discontented masses to shape up into a movement actually had no access to history, nor in truth did it find any when this movement had become, in fact, a political force of major scale. The denial of Christ as "King of the Jews" repeated itself on the plane of world history in the denial by the Christian churches of the political and social problems inherent in the development of the West. The churches proved themselves no more able to stop endless warlike clashes among Christian nations than to make a definitive contribution toward pacifying their own internal social sense.

The real ordering and progressive element of Western history is the humanist tradition of antiquity. This tradition, by virtue of its preservation in Roman law, and because eventually it was again affirmed in the renascence of Greek ideals, came to suffuse Christian spirituality and modify its concentration on the end of the world and a judgment day. Also, working in concert with the pre-Christian social tradition of the Continental peoples, it introduced the period of democracy. Christianity came into fruitful relationship with history and society only whenever and wherever, for reasons of self-interest, it saw itself forced to support and justify existing dominant systems.

If one does not believe that Christianity's stunning success depended solely, or in great measure, on the fact that after Constantine it became a state-religion, then other general psychological reasons must be sought to explain the tremendous synthesis of East and West that came to pass, conditions typical of the fusion of the young Continental peoples into the new world structure. In the early phase of the nascent Continental realm, as it was taking shape in opposition to, and yet in the midst of, the old Mediterranean cultural sphere, a pristine longing, fresh as the morn, arose, a mighty urge to realize Christianity politically and intellectually, to perform deeds of heroism and dominion, to seek moral and religious justification. Christianity had a missionary vocation and

zeal. It was inspired by a passionate will to act, to go into battle for
God's kingdom and glory on earth. Christian morality proved
superior to the tolerant, passively and skeptically inclined ethical
ideas of antiquity essentially because it managed to look beyond
all those limitations of human nature which tended to undermine enthusiasm.

And the fact that Christianity claimed ultimate jurisdiction over
the world of men and cherished a feeling of superiority verging on
intolerance also reinforced this youthfully vital feeling of self-
confidence. It was inevitable that this élan, as Christianity strove
for affirmation and prestige in the here and now, should also tend
to bolster the very concrete allegations of the Christian religion.
The veneration of a purely mystic deity—such as Mithras certainly
was—never could have served to feed the will as it strove to accomplish definite historic tasks. But Christ had been historically witnessed. He was God working in and through history, a deity who
admitted no other gods but himself. The absoluteness of his claim
carried over to his followers and made them into a community
of chosen servants and warriors in Christ. The real history of mankind, it was maintained, had begun with Christ. For peoples in
process of girding their loins to make history, no conception
could have been more apropos.

Thus, the strongly marked individuality of the Christian movement synchronized with the craving for personality among the
masses of antiquity just as they were being set free by the dissolution of older social forms, and at the same time with the need of
barbarian peoples for self-confirmation. Because Christianity offered
a personal god and a personal and immortal soul, in it the individual descried a value unobtainable from the nature cults and
philosophies of antiquity. In the metapersonalism of Christianity
the ego became the most precious and most essential of all things,

because this ego lasted beyond death and contained the key to communication with God. The Christian is charged with tirelessly pursuing the struggle to maintain, most perfectly mold and save the individual soul. This struggle revolving about the individual soul was also a struggle against sin and unbelief, a battle to be carried on in the secure consciousness of possessing the truth. This provided a redemptive escape from the skepticism and cynicism of the decadent Greco-Roman civilization.

And were not the many Christian martyrs, who allowed themselves to be nailed unresisting to the cross, or ripped to shreds by wild beasts, witnesses of the truth and power of their belief? Then, finally, the surface intelligibility and clarity of the Christian model of the world had a fascination for a mankind wearied of a farrago of complicated mythologies and speculative systems. In the beyond was the one great and omnipotent God, and here the world. He had sent Christ as his messenger and Christ had proclaimed what had to be believed and acted on in order to enter paradise. Reduced to this scheme, Christian dogma was bound to appeal to those looking for a simple and practical explanation of the world.

As long as scientific thinking did not develop, there was little difficulty in assimilating Christian ideas of belief, even among peoples of the antique and Continental world who, at bottom, were otherwise disposed. The European peoples, at this stage of the game, were quite unconscious of their own mode of world understanding. European man as yet had evolved no criteria for testing the content of his belief. The thin layer of philosophers, thinkers and savants was in no way representative of the general state of knowledge. The transition to monotheistic Christianity, therefore, ad interim was unquestionably an advance. It was an innovation that widened and lit up the world horizon. The multiplicity of gods and daemons lost their hold on men's minds. Men gained in inner security, freedom and humanity.

Christianity was able to unite with the emergent Continental civilization because it arrived at just the right political and psychological moment in the developmental process. Yet it was also in the cards that some day Christianity would be cast aside. As soon as the natural in Western man had matured to a point where, in its give and take with the environment, it began to evolve a system of scientific truths—a kind of evidence differing in mode from, and irreconcilable with, the postulates of belief—the sloughing off phase was under way. But actually many centuries passed before this occurred, indeed a thousand years and more. For the new faith's militantly transposed ethic, its claim to exclusiveness and universal redemption, its drive to convert and teach, and its high evaluation of the individual, made of Christianity, now additionally permeated as it was with European emotion and ideas—a religious ideology that fitted in with Western needs until late medieval times.

The Crusades to stem the heathen advance were carried out directly under the Christian aegis. At the same time they definitely gave the European knightly ideal a fanatic and brutalized tone. The opposition in this case was not simply an enemy to be quelled, but a servant of the devil accursed of God. Heathen and heretics had a choice between conversion and physical destruction. Little scope was left for fairness or generosity toward the vanquished. That something of the knightly spirit was preserved, however, is shown in the strength of the European military tradition. It was additionally kept alive by the circumstance that most Christian wars were fought among Christian peoples, which of course made for certain mutual concessions. However, even within the Western World the bound between knightly warfare and a fanatical urge to annihilate was repeatedly crossed. Indeed, such a transgression is unavoidable if the militant believe themselves alone to be in possession of the absolute truth and if the enemy's destruction seems to serve this truth. Europeans were similarly able to reconcile the subjugation of alien peoples with Christ's message of love and deliverance. They also used their missionary idea as justification of imperialistic claims and all manner of abominations visited upon the recalcitrant heathen in the process of appropriating their world. And perfectly obvious to this day is the powerful influence of the Crusader ideology in the methods and views of world politics.

In all events, the incorporation of an alien Christian religiosity into the Continental-European character took place in that part of human life which is spontaneously active and kinetic, not in the reflective sphere or phase. At the beginning, at least, it occurred easily, even with great intensity. This European capacity to absorb a foreign creed had its roots in a youthfulness as yet untrammeled by thought, a state of mind much less bent on seeing through the world's scheme than on standing up to it in a spirit of challenge and self-affirmation. Christianity had only an emotional and psychological appeal to the European. And it is in this fact that we find an explanation for the small genotypic configurative strength shown by the real Christian ideal of life throughout the Western World.

To be sure, an alien ideal can influence character in its youthful stage, since at this juncture there is more plasticity. Yet the ideal makes only a limited impression. The Christian impetus was effective only within the foreshortened, superficial and distorted perspective in which it was apprehended. It was like a highly concentrated injection, which set the organism of the Continental peoples, pressing toward self-realization as they already were, into vital reverberation. But this injection did not succeed in striking home to the very core of the European nature. It did not mold its very essence. From the Chrsitian concept of the world and history, European man drew forth only those political, moral and intellectual energies which furthered his release. Its real and basic content was ignored, suppressed or distorted.

5

CHRISTIANITY'S CREATIVE
PROMISE UNFULFILLED

THE DE-CHRISTIANIZATION of the West, the attempt ever renewed to throw off the yoke of the Christian-Paulinist metaphysic, is a phenomenon that first found expression in the Renaissance, in humanism and the Reformation and, ultimately, in the modern European spirit and its persistent tendency to secularize. Basically everything that has stirred the thinking element of Western peoples since the days when Greek philosophy was rediscovered is part and parcel of this broad and continuing process of "enlightenment." At first in trustful conformity with Christian dogma, later apart from but still alongside it, and at last against it, the struggle to achieve enlightenment on the true nature of things has gone on. Using the term "enlightenment" to designate this whole block of intellectual history would be misleading only if it were made to connote—legitimately enough, in general principle—the idea of enlightening whole masses of people or whole social strata. Here

some qualification is necessary. In the early days of Reuchlin and
Erasmus the increase in knowledge and the change of intellectual
temper was limited, in fact, to a small minority of savants and
educated people. In a time marked by almost universal illiteracy
the influence of such people on general religious conviction had to
be small. But the élite who had access to the literature of antiquity
and who were accustomed to the mutual exchange of experiences
and ideas, in due course insensibly led those who thirsted to know
ever deeper into the maze of the knowable and ever farther out of
the snug security of inherited belief.

This process of detachment took centuries to accomplish. A great
deal of time, not to mention special social conditions and a certain
level of civilization, was needed before the insight of the few
became the certainty of the many, and the old beliefs lost their
power to convince not only in the heads of a few scholars but in
peoples' hearts as well. The de-Christianization of the West at first
was an issue fought out in the studies of the learned. Then, when
the time became ripe to print books for the many and to teach
them how to read, and de-Christianization spread naturally as a
result of popular education. At last, when a desire for social justice
spontaneously flowed out of the masses' need spiritually to come of
age—with Christianity meanwhile on the defensive and fighting
both these tendencies—de-Christianization became identified with
and shaped by the process of political development. This movement, meanwhile, was concurrently reinforced by progress in
natural philosophy and its precipitates in literature of all kinds.
But it was not until the last century that the process of religious
breakdown reached a peak. This came about through the populari-
zation of the new anthropological and natural sciences, which cast
fresh light on the essential structure of the world and man.

The conflict inherent in the spirit of the Christian West became visible at an early stage in all its irremediability as Christian and Continental tendencies were interacting to produce the splendors of the Christian-Occidental culture. Medieval philosophy and what then passed as science were for a time content to seek rational proof for dogma as yet basically unquestioned. They functioned according to the premise that what could be thought—God, immortality, freedom of will—by definition could and must exist. Yet this device of forcing believing and knowing into correspondence eventually had to be abandoned, either by denying Christian dogma outright, or by postulating that it consisted of revealed truths inaccessible to reason. Pleading credence for the unreasonable, Christian apologists drew back from the awakening skepticism, and ever since have remained on the defensive.

During the course of the last five centuries ever more revealed "truths" were supplanted by scientific truths, with the result that in the 19th century, when the new knowledge of the biological and physical sciences began to filter through all levels of society, that segment of Western mankind which supplied leadership and decision began to pay only phlegmatic lip-service to Christianity. These people, in their outlook on the world and their feeling for life, long since had been converted to a new kind of "paganism." Still, Western man hesitated for many reasons to admit openly that for him Christianity was becoming less and less condign. He preferred either to keep his heretical thoughts under his hat, or to let them lie safely in works of philosophy, art and science, where their danger to Christianity could only be deviously inferred. In this attitude of caution a serious consideration was the fact that avowing oneself as against Christianity could affect one's very livelihood. Indeed, to this day there are Christian states and cultures in which the dissident risks economic security and social standing, if no longer life and freedom.

Whatever else a superficial consideration of the so-called Christian hemisphere may reveal, this much is true: Anyone who without bias looks over the last thousand years of Western history is forced to the conclusion that Western man, the more his character matured, as he tried to penetrate the world's pattern not only in a practical way but by systematic and interpretative thought, the more he came into irreconcilable conflict with the Christian point of view. The Christian churches themselves bear eloquent witness to this state of affairs. Time and time again they resisted and charged with heresy the great spirits of the Renaissance and the periods of humanism and enlightenment.

The net result of all this is that Christianity has ceased to pervade European-Atlantic life as a molding influence. Very recent attempts to revitalize the Christian ethic by means of "Christian humanism" or "Christian socialism" are no proof to the contrary. A religion which is reduced to defending its ethical solicitation is already moribund. Its name cannot be saved merely by associating it with contemporary aspirations typical of humanity everywhere.

Recently a West German demographic institute, one which is certainly free of any suspicion of atheism, made a survey of modern marriage and family problems. This survey showed that a majority of those questioned still favored the Biblical text, "Whither thou goest, I will go." But only a negligible percentage understood this as a religious and Christian prescript. It was mostly thought of as expressing a desire for a strong personal bond between married people. The investigation came to the general conclusion that only about two-fifths of all persons interrogated had a thoroughly positive attitude toward Christianity. This suggests that certain basic moral injunctions are shared alike by Christianity and any civilized moral system. But the mere fact that such injunctions have currency should not be allowed to conceal the circumstance that they are only incidentally Christian, and not specific evidence of Christianity as such. It is only on the common foundation of all human beings whatsoever, each possessed of individual will, that the diverse systems of metaphysics—polytheist, monotheist and atheist, dualist and monist, dynamic and static—can rise up out of their pluralism into ethical forms applicable to all humanity.

Today the real Christian creed, viewed in the broad, scarcely survives as a vitally creative force. The peoples of the West, as they live out their lives—and this takes into account the majority of those who call themselves Christians—in their thinking and behavior have ceased to pay the least attention to Christianity's idea of God and the hereafter, or the Christian notions of sin and grace. Christianity was once a faith that really pervaded human existence. But it has been supplanted by a kind of indifferent tolerance of that theological phraseology which, every Sunday, resounds from pulpit and loudspeaker. It has come to be accepted as a ritual composed of humanitarian protestations, appeals and activities, pursued by dint of much expensive publicity. We, the inheritors of Western culture, live in the midst of all kinds of testimonials and memories of Christianity, as will many generations to come, and this circumstance still leaves a characteristic mark on our lives. Yet, in this same connection, the bulk of people who busy themselves professionally with the appreciation and evaluation of these Christian memorials are not motivated in truth by religious zeal, but by a mere philological or esthetic interest.

In spite of this epigonal state of affairs it would be false and reprehensible to propagate the destruction of the inherited form and content of the Christian-Occidental culture. For "progress" of this nature would not only disrupt the historical continuum, but at the same time rob the world of the fruits of the past, riches without which neither present nor future can have meaning.

Therefore, it is not so much a question of opposing Christianity as such, as of further awakening a consciousness of the spiritual condition of mankind outside the framework of inherited conviction.

Looking back over the years, we are certainly justified in concluding that none of the ersatz religions—either those tried and found wanting or those still extant, from materialism to psychologism to sociologism—can ever contain reality's plenum of being. At the same time these one-sided and counterfeit movements can be validly adjudged symptomatic of a basic change in the Western-European consciousness. There is no fault to be found with these experiments in the sense that they represent an attempt to bring man and the world into a system based on demonstrable truth. But where they are naïve and false is in their assumption that any new correlation of reality must take, by all means available to the human intellect, the form of a reduction to a common denominator, an ultimate formula acceptable to all. As a matter of fact, in our own times it has been realized that to fill with rational material the "religious" void left by the overthrow of the Christian metaphysic is an impossible task. It is this discovery which holds us in irons, and which has led to a revival of all kinds of antirationalism and subjectivism.

In whatever direction we look, toward philosophy, the arts, literature or science, everywhere minds are hard at work laying bare to view the background and the underground of life, exposing the metaphysical and metapsychical, the magical, the unreal and the beyond-the-real. These analysts, having cut reality ignominiously open on their dissecting table, try to breathe new meaning and mystery into the corpse. Meanwhile, in defensive reaction to this process, others adjure us to open our eyes to this vain and foolish "flight from God," and again seek refuge and safety in the true faith. The whole history of European enlightenment, these people say, is nothing more than a great heresy, a dangerous illusion and overevaluation of man's intelligence. It behooves us, henceforth, to restore Christ's message of redemption to its rightful supremacy, since from this message alone true knowledge and release can come. None but Christ's teachings can control reason's arrogant claims and again commit mankind to lost moral and spiritual values.

Our conviction is quite opposite. It is our belief that the process of transforming and widening the Western consciousness has been a necessary thing, and cannot be reversed. Within this development there may be errors in need of correction. But this does not hold true for the development as such. Not all the results of scientific study can be suddenly judged false simply because certain credulous men of science happen to draw unwarranted inferences from them.

Western man's emancipation from the spiritualistic and dualistic Christian metaphysic is basically characterized by a discovery of the unity of all being, which revelation has spilled over into the general awareness. As the struggle to get to the bottom of all things is pressed farther and farther, the seeking mind comes hard up against the fact that man and all the forces which motivate him and constitute him are part of the continuum of reality. The world cannot be divided into a life on earth and a hereafter. Actually everything contains a "this side" and a "that side." The "this side" turns out merely to be that part of world unity which is accessible to the senses, and "that side" the part of the whole which remains in the dark. The absolute dualism of the Christian concept of the world and the concept of deity linked to it, in this view have been done away with. What remains is the relative dualism of the knowable and unknowable. This simply indicates that a portion of the world lies outside human experience, but not "outside the world."

Today we are witnessing an inescapable breakdown of all forms of speculation and myth derivative from ignorance of reality's true relationships. Meanwhile a need has arisen to project a kind of metaphysic that will go beyond the accumulated facts of experience, yet still be rooted in experience. We find ourselves today in a period where the old and new outlooks overlap. On the one hand we see an attempt to force inductive truth into traditional doctrine; on the other, a need to formulate a system of belief resting easily and naturally on these same demonstrable truths.

Even where Catholicism is still deeply rooted, as in such rural and backward parts of Europe as Spain, or in Latin America, places in which Catholicism is still a state religion seemingly in possession of unlimited power over men's souls, it is doubtful whether on-coming generations will spontaneously accept the Christian tradition and carry it forward in time. And in the highly civilized, dominantly Protestant countries—above all in the United States, the nation which henceforth will lead the Western World—in these countries, where Christianity still holds uncontested sway over the cultural façade, the Christian idea has degenerated into trivial moralism, which has no religious superstructure left at all, and in lieu of it projects the Babbitt ideal, of the man who is in all ways healthy, normal and satisfied with himself, the world and providence. The settlers of the "New World" soon found themselves in a situation not unlike that of the Continental peoples at the time of their encounter with Christianity. There was a great urge to create a new way of life. Indeed, this had to be done. This impulse merged with the individualistic, activist and missionary ideology of Christianity, without, however, greatly exciting any desire to think seriously about the religious and philosophical motivation of this ethic. It is fairly obvious, in this general connection, that the pioneer spirit, as linked with Christian individualism, played an essential part in spreading practical humanitarianism and the democratic way of life. But it is only a half-century ago that the problem of finding an ontologically sound and reasonable foundation for ethic and being began to be discussed in America, whereas in the Old World thinking people had been wrestling with the problem for centuries.

As soon as man begins to live consciously, as soon as he ceases to be guided by imported norms and instead conceives a desire to do and strive, wish and want in terms of his own insight, so that he may bring his life, as he feels, into an intelligible relationship with all reality—when this happens any lack of harmony between motive and deed, idea and configuration, the believed and the known tends to become intolerable. Having arrived at this stage, man must either find new motives while continuing to act as before, or new forms of action while retaining his old motives. That is, he must either find a new way to accommodate his existence to the Christian idea of faith, or rebuild his existence on a non-Christian basis. In the end there is nothing left for him to do but to bring everything that he does, hopes or wishes into harmony with what he has come to believe is the nature of the whole.

Though modern "unbelief" is a deep-reaching, collective phenomenon, the process from which it results is still immature, which in turn limits individual apostasy. It is a gradual thing. The transformation of a "believer" into an "unbeliever" does not threaten to upset the individual's psychic equilibrium, as a rule, since it comes about insensibly from a gradual widening of the consciousness. This process is occurring everywhere. The facts which make for doubt and which force human beings to think things over and form new ideas are reaching out into the remotest villages. These facts come into purview, too, without any special outside assistance. Whether remotely situated people respond to these forces or let them pass in indifference depends, of course, on their relative intellectual and psychological development. The spirit listeth where it will, but bears fruit only on fertile ground. If a genuine desire for enlightenment obtains, contemporary man has only to reach out his hand to satisfy it. If this desire is lacking, better then that he remain secure in his old faith.

As far as prognosis is possible, it seems almost certain that among immediately ensuing generations the structure of consciousness will suffer a fundamental change. This change will occur even among populations still living on the periphery of civilization. The thinking of erstwhile backward and primitive peoples will tend more and more toward the objective. The same prognosis also applies to the peoples of Asia and Africa, though here the collision between enlightenment and traditional religious beliefs, in accordance with the tremendous variety of the latter, very likely will give rise to motley results and bring all sorts of divers consequences to a head. Not only Buddhism but Islam as well contains metaphysical postulates which might very well prove quite serviceable as a superstructure for advancing scientific thought. We have already indicated the compatibility of the Buddhistic world-idea and rational knowledge. Mohammed's message, too, is anti-miraculous, and is characterized by a strong incentive, liable at any moment to be quickened, to make use of man's God-given powers of understanding in praise of creation. Both religions could have a great deal of appeal in the West, if they were skillfully maneuvered. The great conflict among the world's three principal religions has yet to come. There could be a phase of de-Christianization in which Buddhism and Islam might come to be regarded as acceptable substitutes. For men driven to despair will tend first to seek a new meaning for existence in already great and recognized systems of belief.

A small but very active group of intellectuals is currently defending Christian belief in the West. How is their enterprise faring? Their activity is profiting mostly by the tendency, in the modern middle class, to hold fast to and defend the cultural riches to which it is heir. This inclination, of course, is stronger in artistic, esthetic natures than among reflective types. To people of feeling an attack on Christian dogma seems like an attack on the very foundations of Western culture. From their point of view Western culture would be unthinkable without Christianity's distinctive influence.

The cultivated man, in sum, is repelled by the unimaginative and sterile "ideologizing" of modern agnosticism, which offers no occasion for creating or enjoying things of beauty. Thus, in a certain phase of its decline every religion becomes "literature." That is, it tends to make itself esthetically palatable. It promotes itself through drawing attention to the splendor of its cultural deposits and the life-style on which its imprint is ubiquitously discernible, while at the same time refusing to give an accounting of its credal content. Today there are many esthetic apologists for Christianity, the kind of people whose zeal to defend is fired by cathedrals, holy legends and paintings of the Madonna. Such people make no pretense of inquiring into the persuasiveness of the Christian doctrine. For them the esthetic, literary and dramatic richness of Christianity's monuments is enough evidence of truth. In this situation Christianity is thought of as a triumph of the "cultivated" over the "vulgar."

A further explanation of the affinity of esthetic and emotional natures for Christianity lies in the fact that these people—as clearly shown in the history of the Romantic movement—hanker for the ideal, the spiritualized. Personalities strongly governed by emotion tend to place too much emphasis on the spirit. It is considered to be a kind of super- or extra-human attribute, for the reason that emotional man has so much trouble realizing himself spiritually amid the distraction of his impetuous drives. To him spirit seems like something opposed to nature, as in the Christian sense. Moreover, the esthetic person is led, by his false and excessive evaluation of the formal, the proportioned and the playful, to the erroneous conclusion that only those who possess talents along these lines occupy a special and superior place in the world. He inclines to think of the ability to create artistically in a self-sufficient and disinterested way as evidence of a god-like nature.

Therefore, it is no mere accident that religious zeal and proselytism are so common among artists, actors and poets. Christianity's moral relativism may also be a factor in this situation. According to this moral view, the vilest of beings, the worst of cast-offs—indeed, they more than others, by virtue of their degradation—can share in God's grace and become his elect. What man of feeling would not prick up his ears at such a generous message! People who are fascinated by sin and passion are also especially prone to believe these tidings. Then, again, the mystery of the Virgin Birth not only has an arcane and esthetic appeal for the sensitive man, but attracts him, too, as a promise of redemption "through faith alone." He is drawn, in other words, simply because his capacity to believe is challenged.

In this general connection we can hardly overlook the fact that Catholicism more than any other creed, in certain areas of the middle class, attracts and bolsters up the ego of a kind of human being who is exceedingly arrogant and snobbish. This kind of person actually is the precise opposite of the Christian apologist who operates from a moral point of view. Whereas the ethical apologist, remote as he may be from the specific content of

Christian belief, defends Christian dogma since he fancies that morality would collapse without it, in the hands of the snob the Christian metaphysic becomes nothing but a corpus of wisdom, permitting the world to be viewed from an esoteric, esthetic and dramatic standpoint that lends its adherents a contemplative and spiritualistic nimbus. This mundane version of Christianity, however, is a sign of the lateness of the hour. Forced onto the defensive by the skepticism of an awakening consciousness, all the esthetes and dilettantes, the immoralists and the snobs, rush to the barricades to do battle for their worldly Christian concept. But in the end the net result is artistic formalism, an attitude evidencing intelligence and taste, but devoid of inner sympathy and power of faith. It lends the sunset splendor, but does not guarantee the dawn. Neither the intellectual rear-guard of Christian revival, nor those who for political reasons make common cause with the Christian church, nor yet peasant elements as yet untouched by the enlightenment process will ever usher in a new medievalism.

6

THE PERIOD OF ERSATZ RELIGIONS

SERIOUS MISDEVELOPMENTS inevitably resulted from the fact that Continental man's natural, world-directed inclination was smothered by an overlay of a world-blind and world-hostile Christian metaphysic. Powers of understanding suppressed and held in contempt for centuries at last broke free. Exaggerated claims were made for the validity of the rational. "The hubris of reason"— beloved theme of contemporary philosophers—was the immediate and inescapable consequence of Christianity's hostility toward the intellect. When a man has had to live and act against his own nature for a long period, he will, as soon as he gets a chance to function unhindered, very easily fall into the trap of overestimating his own point of view and his own criteria. This reaction is all the stronger, too, when reason emancipated still does not have complete freedom of utterance. At any rate, once the European had come to recognize the value of rational thought and had confirmed it through the splendid achievements of science and technology, he began to show signs of a dangerous tendency to reject everything that contradicted reason, or which was above it. His need to ensure just due for the "ratio"—the reckoning or thinking faculty—led him greatly to overshoot the mark. He carried self-justification to extremes. Throwing off the shackles of theological tutelage, he not only disputed the ultimate impotence of man's reasoning power as alleged by Christianity, but went a step beyond this to maintain there was nothing between heaven and earth inaccessible, over the long run, to human understanding. And in view of the fact that Christianity itself had lodged the idea in the European mind that the irrational and the beyond-the-rational were identical, it was now erroneously imagined that by unmasking the first, the second had been obviated.

As we have said before, Western man is governed by an innate desire for enlightenment. Galileo Galilei's astronomical discoveries, Nicolas of Cusa's break with scholasticism, the Copernican cosmogony, the discovery of America, Gutenberg's movable type, the Darwinian theory, the theories of Marx, Freud and Einstein, the splitting of the atom and electronics—all these are so many way-stations on the great highroad to enlightenment. With the Europeanization of Western man and a shift of the intellectual center of gravity from the Mediterranean to the west and north of Europe, the scientific period had been ushered in. Henceforth men were no longer content merely to believe and live in belief. They wanted to know.

The instrument of this will to knowledge, the weapon, sharpened in a thousand passages-at-arms, which Continental man used to attack and vanquish the world, was a highly developed intellect. With its help he penetrated through the surface of things and unlocked nature's secrets. Ever more exact investigations disclosed life's many-layered structure. Ever more complex systems of lawfulness came to hold existence fast. There seemed to be nothing left which, given time, would not be weighed and measured. The magic formula had been found. The day was not too far off when the last riddle would be solved.

This expectation proved illusory. Life, in all its forms of appearance, is more than a mere experimental object illuminable by reason. Life can never be completely understood. It is rationally accessible only up to a point. However, in order to support the illusion of having laid hold of the "other part," thus ensuring a grip on the "whole," the lawfulness governing the graspable structure of reality was arbitrarily made to govern all. Grasses and animals, rocks and seas, stars and human beings ceased to be thought of as forms of existence rising up out of an unknowable substrate and continually reaching down into this fundament. They were now thought of in terms of substances and processes that could be completely reduced to a measurable system of quantities and relationships. The world took on the appearance of a network of processes, exceedingly intricate yet thoroughly understandable. What was discovered through and for reason was *ipso facto* valid for the totality of being. This radical scientization was an inadmissible simplification, the leveling out of what in fact was a multidimensional reality into one of two or three dimensions. The scientific mind's characteristic tendency to abstract single levels out of a hierarchized totality and to study them in their particularity led to the isolation of these strata and so to the illusion that whereas they might not, indeed, be the whole itself, nevertheless they were a key to the knowledge of the whole. Each monocausalism tended to confuse general concepts derived from the investigation of partial spheres with principles lawful for all existence. The uncritical need to find one, ultimate, all-ruling formula, in view of the limitations of human reasoning power, necessarily led to the hypostasis of partial truths. And precisely on

account of this inflationary process ever more partial truths came
to be apprehended, which in turn were blown up into the last
word in scientific novelty.

But the responsibility for the tendency of modern thought limit-
lessly to believe in facts, a trend which Christianity has especially
lamented and reviled, in cold truth falls squarely into the lap of
none other than Christianity itself. Christianity had preempted and
kept a grip on the religious sphere by all-or-nothing, totalitarian
methods. This was bound to impress on the consciousness of Western man the idea that whatever was religious in nature must be
like Christianity. In any event, as the absurdity of the Christian
dogma became increasingly evident, resulting in alienation from
the faith, the sense of religiosity itself began to disappear. The
anti-Christian temper of the 17th, 18th and 19th centuries developed into actual irreligiosity. The great rationalists and cultural
apostles of the age, meanwhile, mistook their distaste for the monstrous speculations of Christian theology as evidence that religious
feelings and religious ideas of any kind were superfluous. This
fateful misapprehension must be appreciated in all its consequences,
for it provides the key to understanding, in all its alarming qualities, the recent history of the culture of the West. Man, in sum,
fell into a state of chronic confusion, from being unable to har-
monize what he knew to be true with what he imagined he ought
to believe. He began to suffer, and still suffers to this day, from a
crippling of his ability to integrate, a defect which has all the ear-
marks of a severe neurosis.

The character of Western man exhibits a whole syndrome of
pathological symptoms, collaterally derivative from a misapplication
of the Christian ideal of life. But the superficiality, unrest and
monomania so strikingly typical of modern thought and behavior
are the immediate result of the insoluble conflict between re-

vealed and rational truths. The umbilicus by which mankind is attached to the world-whole and the world-substrate, and thus to the essence of his being, has been severed. Once the metaphysical superstructure breaks away, all that remains of a now dichotomized world is the mundane half, by God forsaken. This lower half must carry the additional burden of everything formerly supported by belief. Christianity's claim that it is "the" religion—which unbelievers never think to dispute—meanwhile residually prevents conjecture about the possibility that another religious approach can and eventually must evolve. Thus, defection from Christianity has a narrowing and impoverishing effect, and reality degenerates into mere actuality. The human gaze slides restlessly over the surface of things, pausing here and there to lay hidden mechanisms bare. The end result of it all is the elevation of physical principles to the status of final truths. Because Christianity blocks off access to the discovery of universal meanings, the world tends to disintegrate into a multiplicity of phenomena, which can, to be sure, be tied together logically, but which can never really be brought under a single meaning superior to and comprehending the whole.

Continental man would never have arrived at such a profound alienation from self if, out of the mode of life into which he was born, he had been allowed spontaneously to develop a "religion" offering unity of experience and belief. Scientific thought does not of its own accord lead to scientistic superstition, materialism and positivism. Moreover, why should science not pretend to metaphysical insights, if these insights do not contradict experience, but pull it together and justify it? The truth is, if scientific thought could unfold without coming into conflict with residual forms of belief, a clear paraconsciousness would develop spontaneously and become the source of genuine and fruitful philosophical reflection. This is demonstrated by the intellectual life of all scientists and thinkers who have sought after the truth before or independently of Christianity. The overwhelming majority of their Christian-Occidental colleagues, however, have squandered their energies in a useless attempt to effect a reconciliation on the "religious" issue, or have ignored it altogether.

The as yet unresolved conflict with the Christian metaphysic that is typical of modernity has led to such a drastic suppression of the "religious" need that mankind has tended to lose sight of everything beyond reason's range. A flight into fact has resulted. And wherever doubt has arisen about the power of science completely to account for the phenomena of existence, the nascent religious need has been promptly stifled by the impossible demands of the Christian dogma. Meanwhile, in answer to the final, eschatological questions Christianity offers a system of events and speculations so manifestly fantastic that any serious discussion of it would be as pointless as trying to explain *Alice in Wonderland* in terms of physical credibility. If "having religion" and "being religious" means accepting pious legend as history and theological constructs as objective statements of fact, then religion becomes an impossibility. It is for this reason that man has been driven to concentrate on the trustworthy, provable facts of recorded history and science.

In whatever direction he looked, modern man was confronted by the irrefragable lawfulness of events. Whatever might be the object of his investigation—the movements of heavenly bodies, physical and chemical events, biological and psychological processes —it was found to be governed by necessity. The earth, man discovered, was not the center of an endless cosmos, but a mere speck of dust within it. Creation was not to be explained away as a week's work by a demiurge. On the contrary, it was the result of astronomical events occurring spontaneously throughout unimaginably long periods of time. As for man, he had appeared on this planet as the last link in a long chain of evolution, beginning with simple organic substances and continuing through the fishes, reptiles and mammals. This kind of world harbored no possibility of "aboveness" or "outsideness." The cosmic processes rolled on autonomously. It seemed senseless to postulate the intervention of supernatural, extra-mundane forces in this situation. Though no one could comprehend the entire multiplicity of the cosmos, reality's manifold structures gave every sign of being a faultlessly interwoven mechanism, inclusive of all things imaginable, organic and inorganic.

The unknown, to be sure, remained unknown. But there was never any reason to believe that unpredictability and lawlessness might suddenly crop up in some unexplored, or as yet incompletely explored, realm of being, thus permitting a point of departure for daemonic events and interventions, for sorcery and magic. All that ever had been, had been thus and so of necessity, and not because of divine or diabolic intervention. The whole world feeling of the closing years of the 18th, and of the entire 19th, centuries was governed by the conviction that more and more of the unknown in due course would be transformed into the known. The solution of whatever mysteries remained could only be a question of time. This belief in the unconditional and comprehensive validity of the causality principle and in the capacity of human reasoning power to track down life's most recondite events resulted in the development of what have been called "ersatz religions."

Every human being, every people, every historical epoch seeks to find a universal answer to the question of what is life's essence and meaning. When a defection from inherited ideas of belief occurs, they are replaced by general principles governing the realm of experience as man then apprehends experience. These principles are presumed to provide meaning for all being. It is in this general fashion that substitute religions arise, following the abandonment of existing religion grown stale. It is when a religion shows itself to be unbelievable that superstitious substitutes arise. A really convincing world-design—one that premises neither scientific knowledge nor philosophical sophistication—is able to hold its own no matter how far the borders of human experience are extended. If it is able to convince, it need never suffer embarrassment through comparison with substitute religions. However, it so happens that the European mind's lamentable drift toward a variety of pseudo-ideologies during the past 150 years and its lopsided dedication to material interests, technical perfection and shallow distractions can be traced back to the decay of the Christian faith. When Christianity no longer offered a convincing meaning for life, in its place "ideologies" appeared which based their claim to credibility on "facts." Facts suitable for making over into general principles were found in two realms of experience: the objective world of things and the unique inner world of human beings.

It was the lawfulness governing all environmental phenomena that was first revealed to man's searching gaze. This lawfulness was relatively easy to observe and prove. Astronomy, physics and chemistry were the first sciences to give mankind an objective knowledge of the structure of reality. They were followed by biology as a system of lawfulness governing the organic, then by the historical and social sciences as epitomes of factors broadly determining human life. Individual man, however, and the drives, tendencies and ideas determining his inner being, long after the first efflorescence of the natural and historical sciences, continued to be a literary and broadly philosophical theme, rather than an object of scientific research. Man, the individual, was discovered belatedly by science because, as a scientific subject, he was extraordinarily complex and hard to penetrate, and knowledge about him presumed a great variety of experience in many sciences. Moreover, there was a certain timidity about coming to grips with events which would inevitably cast doubt on man's godlike nature. On this account the "objective ersatz religions" from the mechanistic cosmology to sociologism, are both much older and much more influential than their "subjective" counterparts. It is the objective ideologies which first appeared as Christianity's power to convince began to wane.

A clear distinction can be made between objective and subjective kinds of religiosity. Those substitute religions which exhibit a fascination for the lawfulness of phenomena environmentally surrounding and conditioning man neglect to account for the interior life of the human person. On the other hand, substitute religions created by observers of interior psychological events tend to ignore the material, biological and sociological relationships in which man is embedded. And both types, each according to the limitations of its perspective, ignore the question of man's position in the cosmos. From either of these pseudo-religious points of view this man-versus-cosmos issue has no significance. The objective systems reduce life's meaning to man's participation in scientific or quasi-scientific processes, whereas subjective ideologies see life's meaning in the unfolding of individual man's ability to experience and enjoy. The objective systems close their eyes to the individual's private fate and the subjective ones to the external factors of existence by which he is inescapably conditioned. Both shirk the problems which man must unremittingly try to solve in order to understand his existence within the cosmic frame.

All ersatz religions behave as if there were no world structure reaching out beyond man's world, as if human existence were completely summed up in biological adaptation, in the historico-social function, or in individualistic-psychic fulfillment of self. At a certain stage in scientific development, namely, with the advent of scientific psychology, objective and subjective attempts at cosmic interpretation come together in theory. Yet practically speaking they do not. Following the development of a scientific psychology, and on into the present, we see two general types of ersatz religion at work—one stressing the environment, the other the individual's inner life. These types, as we have noted, are clearly differentiated.

The new anthropology which even now is in process of taking shape, and which represents the first systematic attempt to utilize both the natural and the social sciences in its study of man's nature, so far has achieved hardly a single noteworthy result, not even in point of publicity or literature, let alone in point of ideology. The great synthesis which some day will serve mankind as the point of intersection and medium of all life's operative relationships, the biological as well as the ideological, the climatic and economic as well as the historical and social, is a task that must be fulfilled by generations yet to come. We can only hope that this panoramic triumph will occur at a stage of intellectual development in which mankind's need for a "religious" accommodation is again recognized. For the scientific synthesis offers no escape of any kind from the blind alley of ersatz religion. Even if a true synthesis did not clarify the religious question, it would at any rate lead to an anthropologism whose ideological claims would be convincing to the extent that they represented a horizontal universality in the interpretation of existence.

This, then, is the situation. The Christian metaphysic's power to convince has greatly diminished, but this diminution has not led Christianity to relinquish its hold on the religious sphere. As a result mankind is seeking comprehensive interpretations in all spheres, anything that seems dependable and credible. Philosophy is still much too dependently involved with theology and much too strongly pervaded by feelings of piety ever to succeed in smashing through the roadblock thrown up by Christian dogma in its retreat. From this source clear insight into cosmic relationships cannot be expected. Indeed, there is no immediate prospect of any scheme of belief squarely confronting the world as a whole. The period of ersatz religions is still in full force.

7

NOTES ON THE THEME OF OBJECTIVISM

OBJECTIVE SUBSTITUTE RELIGIONS are a true mirror image of scientific history. The theory of philosophic mechanism proceeded logically out of classical physics, as surely as biologism was generated by botany and zoology and sociologism by the social sciences and economics. What happens is this: the scientific spotlight falls on some new sector of reality. The secrets of a new and hitherto unknown sphere of life are opened up to the age. So fascinating are these revelations for a time that it seems as if the philosopher's stone had at last been found, the key to everything yet to be understood. If we consider in retrospect how enthusiastically and passionately the contemporary world greeted each successive stage of scientific disclosure and how ardent was the resulting attempt to net the world in the new system of coordinates, we must admit that this characteristic reaction is not without its heroic aspect. Certainly it shows how strong is man's urge to give existence an all-inclusive meaning.

Three facts emerge from a summary scanning of the history of objective ersatz religions. First, a distinction must be made between those derivative from the natural and those from the social sciences. Second, whereas these two types may coexist, each has its characteristic "great period." Third, in more recent times a fusion and concurrence of both types have become noticeable, whereby the end-products of this intermingling, however diverse they may be, all share the common characteristic of being clearly different from all subjective pseudo-religious forms. We also observe, in our survey, that as the masses enter into history, the sociologistic type of ideology pushes into the foreground, while at the same time tending to confirm a complementary theory based on the more exact sciences.

If we conceive modern democracy as born of liberal thinking, and the roundelay of sociologistic pseudo-religions as born of liberalism, we then see how, of necessity, a cultural program arises out of political and economic theory, one that stands in conscious opposition to Christianity and supports the secularization of man's whole outlook on the world. Liberal "thoughts" evolve into "liberalism," which in turn makes common cause with vitalistic and Darwinian theories. Thus liberalism takes on two faces. One looks toward political goals and is expressive of idealism and the desire for freedom; the other toward economic goals, and is expressive of anarchistic materialism. By uniting the assumption that "everything which bears the human visage" has innate dignity and the right to be free, with the conviction that life is "the survival of the fittest," liberalism became effective in a vast field of human experience. At the same time, however, it forfeited the possibility of developing a closed system, and so was preserved from the fate of hardening into an effective ersatz religion. Nevertheless, liberalism is still the mother of all sociologisms. For it was with the advent of liberalism that the social and economic aspects of human existence for the first time moved center-stage in the general consciousness.

The two-sidedness of liberalism also has its tragic aspect. Its powerful humanistic impulse, which introduced a tremendous caesura of world-historical importance into the political thought and behavior of all Western peoples, awoke the masses out of their ignorance and resignation only to dash their hopes in the end. The historical situation in which liberalism was born was governed by trends too strong for humanitarianism to cope with. Liberalism became the ideology of the acquisitive bourgeoisie, the class which, once freed from the feudal system of social estates, introduced the period of capitalism and looked upon the struggle to increase the power of production as analogous to the biological struggle for existence. The "unfit," that is, the great masses of mankind, were left in the ruck. This contradiction generated the social tensions of the early capitalistic period, from which, in due course, evolved the real ersatz religion of the century—communism. A legitimate child of liberal and democratic thought, it revealed the immanent falseness of historical liberalism as it methodically developed and applied what originally had been the humanistic point of departure and humanistic goals. Through communism liberalism has been revealed as a betrayal of the liberal idea. This fighting word, liberalism, became conclusive and convincing at the very moment when it was becoming clear that the biological interpretation of economic and social events in actual fact was nothing more than a scientifically indefensible "justification ideology." It was discovered that the struggle for existence was not a natural socio-economic law. Its philosophic misapplication was no more than a means of glorifying a moral system which permitted men ruthlessly to elbow their way to success. Some came to believe that by denying that the law of survival was applicable to the social sphere, and by no other way, could reason and humanity impress order, planfulness and control on the economic realm.

It was the demonstration, by scientific means, that economic as well as physical processes can be penetrated and their consistency revealed which converted the humanist hopes of liberalism into the pseudo-religious creed and program of communism. Unhampered by the necessity of having to adjust to existing circumstance, communism was able to develop a closed system of interpretation and prediction completely enveloping the life of the individual and of mankind. This ability completely to possess a definite realm of being, the historico-social aspect of life, and to do this without inner contradiction, made an ersatz religion of communism. Its universalist conception engendered such a strong willingness to believe that it was able to absorb the millennial ideas, the element of historical salvation, of Christianity, now in process of disintegration.

It is not any metaphysical claim on the part of Marx and Engels, but the ideological impotence of Christianity that accounts for the fact that socialism, as it developed under pressure from the masses' wish to believe, took on a religious coloration and became what we call "communism." It was not the inborn brutishness or malignity of the European worker, but the Christian church's inability to find credible answers to final questions and to make up its mind to enhance social progress which produced the totalitarian pseudo-religion of communism.

Abandoned by their political, intellectual and religious leaders, the lost sheep came to bank all hope and belief on the coming earthly paradise of the classless society, precisely as once before the masses of antiquity had staked everything on the promise of a paradise in the hereafter. The proposition, so often heard, that the socialist theoreticians promoted the de-Christianization of the masses out of sheer ill will is turning the facts of the case upside down. This idea is one of the most grandiose perversions of historical truth of all time. No level or class ever abjures its own faith, if this faith provides a convincing interpretation of existence and lives up to its claims. Since Christianity could not do the first, it also failed in the second. In fear of losing their power positions the protagonists of Christianity allied themselves with worldly greatness at the expense of justice. The more Christianity lost its ability to convince, the more it became intent upon securing its position as a privileged social establishment. And there was always room for this mistaken tactic, since it was possible to interpret the Christian ethos in terms of a message of love directed toward man's "soul," and as such in no way related to man's longing for happiness here on earth.

From the ground up, socialism has been an attempt to find solutions for historical conflicts, rather than for conflicts inherent in human existence. Socialism is not inclined as such toward secularization and communism. Neither of these things happens through socialism where man's religious ties remain intact. An example of this is modern Burma. Burma is both a socialistic and a Buddhistic country. Yet the leaders of the socialist party, the prime minister and the masses who make up the party have remained Buddhists. The party's thoroughly revolutionary and socialist program has not become inflated into a totalitarian ideology and the sense of the religious sphere's priority has not been lost. The vitality of inherited belief in this country minimizes the possibility that an ersatz religion will arise. Burma, to be sure, may be something of an exception, to the extent that the classic form of Buddhism has been retained there in all purity for centuries. Nevertheless, it is also a fact that in all the other countries of east Asia Buddhism is a guarantee, wherever its influence is felt, against susceptibility to socialism in its totalitarian and pseudo-religious guise. Buddhism will not only withstand the impact of modern science. It will, in addition, be the only great religion to hold fast over the years against communism as an ideological substitute.

Communism has not only left its theoretical mark on the Christian world, but has become a reality in what was once a Christian country. Whereas, in this regard, it is true that this came to pass among a people marked by a peculiar readiness and capacity to believe, it must also be acknowledged that the ideological, historical and moral impotence of Christianity as represented by the Eastern Church disappointed man's expectations with particular thoroughness. Religions do not collapse at the behest of a handful of radicals and intellectuals. They collapse when they prove unable to permeate society and provide the individual with a *point d'appui* to help him cope with the problems posed by his particular time and country. It is obvious that the civilizing influence of Byzantine Christianity, such as it was, was unable to endow Russia with the strength needed to overtake the west European countries that had been experiencing social and material progress for centuries. The unshackling of the practical intelligence resulting from Bolshevism is understandable only if seen as a movement directed against the innate passivity of the Russian character and against the mystic, God-resigned piety of Eastern Christianity which propagated, justified and provided symbols for this given passivity. The passionate unworldliness of the "Russian soul" could be forced to serve progress only by an enormous exaggeration of the rational. The scientization and regimentation of Russian life has been carried to extremes because Russian scientific thought and political reasoning and planning lacked tradition.

Everything developed in Russia in the intellectual realm is contrapuntal in nature and always in danger of dialectic excess. It is anything but astonishing, therefore, that the objective and normative should be overvalued when we consider that the Russians are a people of such unbridled subjectivism. The radicalization and absolutizing of virtues complementary to Christian virtues could only have been prevented by a religion able to absorb and enhance the development of the democratic, scientific and technological tendencies of the age. For these innovations were in any case about to flood into Russia. However, this task Eastern Christianity was singularly unfitted to accomplish. In consequence critically important elements of the bourgeois and petit-bourgeois intelligentsia of Russia pulled away from the church and so from religion altogether.

Certain features of the Russian renunciation of the "soul" in favor of an uncompromising form of "order thinking" (*Ordnungsdenken*) can also be seen in the German sphere, in both Prussianism and National Socialism. The process by which general principles of social behavior such as sense of duty, obedience, loyalty and unselfishness become accentuated into a pseudo-religion as the strength of inherited belief wanes can be very clearly traced out in German life. To be sure, the connections among the manifold perversions in the character structure of European peoples are yet to be investigated in detail. But analysis will almost certainly show that the "de-Christianization" of the West—by which is meant not so much a loss of faith as the intellectual and moral abuse of it—basically derives from the failure of Christianity itself, and not from the failure of Western man.

Treating historical or biological relationships as absolutes is possible only where the real absolute has been lost sight of. Nationalism, too, is a sign of religious fatigue. It is the ersatz religion of the romantic who has lost his faith. The nationalist's concern, as distinguished from the socialist's, is not the creation of a just social order and the lifting up of the level of civilization, but the glorification of history. The nationalist offers up his ability and his claim to self-determination not in the interest of social progress, but of advancing a community of the same blood and language. People of this stripe exhaust themselves, as they search for life's meaning, in trying to maintain, enrich and in all ways enhance this community by whatever means, good or bad, may lie at hand.

Fascism and National Socialism have shown the excesses of thought and deed of which this form of ersatz religion is capable. Nationalism can appropriate literary, historical and scientific motifs, all together or one after the other. "Folk personalities" are discovered, providing a golden opportunity for the romantic poet to play up the state's heroic experiences, happy or unhappy, throughout the course of centuries. The patriotic historian is also given his chance. Meanwhile the theoreticians and propagandists of racism draw supportive argument from zoology and so doing they go several steps beyond the liberals, who resort to zoology merely to justify their economic theories. Among the Nazi and Fascist racists a twisted version of Darwinism became the basis for a social theory. It was the only possible way to cement together a philosophy fraught with the bestial. The characteristic striving of all sociological ersatz religions likewise to seek confirmation in biological and physical science also comes clearly to light in this same instance. The general principle if need be is deliberately torn out of context, since it is the scientific idea alone which now has the power to convince after the religious idea has failed.

It is no mere coincidence that the question of developing man humanistically rather than in terms of nationality or membership in a cultural group should come to a head at the moment in world history when we are witnessing the emergence of a universal anthropology representing a synthesis of all the various sciences. According to this humanistic view nothing less than a knowledge of all divers conditions of subjectivity and individuality among mankind will make it possible to achieve conditions ideal for all men whatsoever and gradually to develop the consciousness that such ideal conditions do potentially exist. A world-state uniting all men under equal, and equally good, circumstances will remain a utopian project until a definition has been arrived at concerning the extent to which the objectively given conditions of individual man's existence are recognizable as such, and as such open to alteration. This is the case quite apart from the political difficulties which will block the realization of a world-state for a long, long time to come. To be sure, man has remained biologically the same for a very long while, and in this sense the stage is set for a world-state. But the assimilation and elevation of today's cultures, races and peoples into a single humanity even as an ideal is unthinkable except under the premise that all national and cultural "holy things" be secularized, with this secularizing process gradually diminishing as the binding power of the great religions is concomitantly reduced.

Only when it has become common knowledge that the uniqueness of each people, race and culture can be traced back to geographical and historical circumstance can a wish be developed among mankind to live together in humanity. As matters stand today it is hardly possible to imagine such an awareness and wish, for even the so-called civilized peoples of the earth conceive their particular configuration and history to be a kind of mystic givenness for which they, personally, can somehow take credit. They do not understand themselves as the product of a particular set of circumstances. Even now the peoples of Asia and Africa are embarking on a period of nationalism which, from the standpoint of world history, will soon be overtaken by the tendencies and ideas of the modern, industrialized mass society, which in turn must lead to another reversion to cosmopolitanism. Present chances of having a world culture are as slim as having a world religion. A world civilization can exist only in correspondence with a world ideology. And both, when and if they come, will be an expression of a higher development of the human race—this contrary to the expectations of the cultural philosophers of conservative kidney who make a career of pessimism.

Meanwhile, however, the civilization of the West shapes up at least as a precursor of world civilization, currently under the spell of a trend toward pseudo-religious absolutism. The opinion we so often hear expressed that a kind of kinship and similarity exists between the American and Soviet mentality is justified, to the extent that the development of both peoples is viewed under the aspect of their mutual drift toward a supremely rationalized way of life, into which many quasi-religious problems have been transferred by Christianity's deterioration. Events set in motion in Russia under duress came about spontaneously in North America, so, too, more and more today in the other countries of the West. The values of a way of life in which the social, scientific and technical themes are strongly emphasized, and the thinking and striving of people dominated by these themes, must at the same time assume the burden of religious need. As the metaphysical understanding retrogresses, civilization as such becomes saddled with pseudo-religion. Striking differences between the Bolshevist dictatorship and the American democracy do of course exist. Yet they cannot disguise the fact that under the ideological auspices of both systems a very similar kind of human stunting and superficiality, a cult of expertise and industry has developed, and that this circumstance can be traced back to the lack of a credible ideology overlapping Western man's whole social and historical existence.

Whereas "collectivism" can be thought of as a system that sacrifices the individual and his private, subjective existence in the interest of ensuring society's smooth functioning, American life can be considered the prime example of conformism, that is, of the urge never to stand out as different, never to do or think unlike anyone else, with the difference that here the sacrifice has been voluntary. And the coercive belief in the promise of the future which is characteristic of Bolshevism seems to be nothing more than a Russian and totalitarian variant of American optimism and belief in progress in the democratic style. It is the narrowing down of life's purview to the problems, products and hopes of the civilizing process which leads historically to an overvaluation of the future and socially to an overvaluation of the collectivity. In this situation attempts to live individualistically lose incentive and justification. Any claim to priority for the theme of individual self-determination can be raised and understood only where a vertical "religious" bindingness is superposed above the horizontal social bindingness.

It is man's lonely struggle to find answers to the great questions of love and death, of time, space and life in their ultimate unknowableness, which releases him from the shackles of collectivism and conformism, and which, in so doing, invests the sphere of what are purely civilizational problems with appropriate meaning. By nature man is irrevocably a social creature and as such obligated to take part in the process of political and civilizational advance. But he is more than a social creature, too. Whether moved by private thought or outside suggestion, his suppressed religious strivings flow into political, social, scientific and technical action and lead him into all the romantic and sadistic, eschatological and materialistic, anarchistic and collectivist distortions of thought and behavior which we have come to know in the past fifty years.

Together with those obsessed by society and civilization the period of ersatz religions has generated many cosmosophists and devotees of *élan vital*, the believers in nature and life as a biological process. These people also belong in the objective school of substitute religions. However, among them we do not so much find a transfer of biological categories to historical events, or a secularization of historical and social theory arising from this transfer, as a direct widening-out of scientific experience and findings to include reality's total structure. In this expansion of the scientific, meanwhile, historic, social and civilizational events come to have only a peripheral interest. This general process begins with the so-called mechanistic concept of the world, according to which the cosmos is understood as a great machine subject to physical and chemical regulation. It ends in the theories of the neo-mystics, who trace back the nature and working of all things to mysterious and magical substances and supernatural powers.

That mode of viewing which sees unity in all being, an approach nourished by the great pantheistic stream of European intellectual history, and confirmed by the findings of the physical and biological sciences, here undergoes, by false simplification, a transformation into an optimism that levels out all the undeniable paradoxes of human existence. Since nearly all these intellectual movements are consciously opposed to Christianity, they succumb to an attempt to disavow the entire Christian metaphysic, together with all its dualist and theocentric speculation. At the same time they try to avoid giving recognition to the psychological facts on which the Christian teachings on sin and redemption are based. Thus a shallow and sentimental idealism develops, devoid of any insight into the multiformity of existence and the conflicts grounded in this multiformity. From this outlook the world and life become a matter of computation, which unfolds harmoniously and is bare of knotty problems, a process in which neither events beyond man's reasoning power nor the tragic have any place. Here there are only errors and failures of execution, and these can be avoided by sensible handling and planning, or on the basis of accurate knowledge or the application of occult powers. But the one factor which constitutes man's specifically human character, his immurement within situations that in truth can never be resolved, is either overlooked or denied.

Every substitute religion is fed from two sources: from the inadmissible extension of half-knowledge to all realms of existence of whatever kind or structure; and the assumption that a formulable meaning is possible for existence. The second aspect, however, is found only in the full-blown type of ersatz religion—the closed system of a rational interpretation of existence. Christianity derives a belated authority from the fact that belief in the possibility of creating such a system is mere superstition, and has proved itself to be such. Meanwhile, however, Christianity hides the fact that it is itself the progenitor of the naïvely rationalistic type of world interpretation. For it has never once dreamt of allowing the indescribable to remain undescribed. On the contrary, Christianity has always claimed to be in possession of a knowledge that solves all enigmas and provides a formulable and total insight into cosmic events. Christianity, indeed, is the prototype of the positivist ideology.

8

NOTES ON THE THEME OF SUBJECTIVISM

OUR ASSUMPTION OF a cleavage in post-Christian ersatz religions into objective and subjective categories is based on the fact that human beings are characterized by two fundamental types. To meet the objection that this would be an unreasonable simplification, and that actually mixed types dominate reality, we can think, perhaps, in terms of preponderance, with one group of human beings preponderantly outward-directed and another inward-directed. This division would correspond to the extroverted and introverted types of conventional psychology. Scientists, technologists and practical people of all kinds belong to the first type, artists and artistically minded persons to the second. Naïve people, that is, the great mass of mankind, all belong in the first category. Remembering that the outward-directed man is largely responsible for the exploration of nature and the impressing of form on human existence, we see that the objectivists have the much greater historico-social significance. The much greater importance of the outward-directed is particularly evident in times of great social upheaval and technical progress.

However, the significance of the subjectivist and individualist, even in our era, should not be underestimated. Most of those who set the tone of philosophy, literature and art, and who give contemporary culture its characteristic impress, feel themselves identified with the subjective camp. Without in the least minimizing Western society's materialist-collectivist tendencies, we recognize that it is still extensively governed by the spiritual-feudal factor. Through students of culture of all ranks the value-giving process filters down into the petit-bourgeois and working classes. This leads to a constant interaction, as far as the general character and broad workings of our culture are concerned, of the naïvely objectivist and the conventionally subjectivist tendencies. Nevertheless, the two camps are still clearly separated. Indeed, a deep hostility, cutting across all social levels, exists between the objectivists and the subjectivists. The subjectivists feel that all attempts to tie them down to objectivist norms are an assault on their personal freedom. The objectivists, on the other hand, view their opposites' predominant concentration on private and subjective concerns as a threat to the social order.

European subjectivism has a multilayered history. Two of its main lines of development have occurred in philosophy and literature. The subterranean and hidden, but bitter, conflict between modern Western philosophy and Christian theology has led, for instance, to the discovery that in Christianity certain religious views had quite obviously arisen through a naïve transference to the divine sphere of human feelings and modes of behavior. While the objectivists were discovering that there was simply no more room in the world for the personal and autonomous God of Christian representation, the subjectivists were revealing that the Christian idea of God was nothing more than a sublime projection of human attributes. Thereafter it was only a short step to the conclusion

that all notions made by man about the oneness and interrelated-
ness of the universe must be nothing more than the product, vary-
ing of course from time to time, of subjective conflict between individuals or groups and the "world." In other words, actually the
"world" and what was thought about it, both proceeded from the
human mind. Thus the ego and the world finally came to merge
and could no longer be held apart. Everything about which it was
possible to make an affirmative proposition, everything that contained meaning and orientation, was now thought of as reflecting
human experience. Thus the pantheistic idea suffered an inversion.
Man and the universe were not a divine idea; on the contrary, God
and the universe were products of human thinking. The problem
of defining objective situations outside the ego-experience was now
explained away as meaningless and naïve. What the objectivists
and realists held to be real in truth was nothing but a reflection of
subjective events, dreams which at the very best could be assigned
no more than a symbolic meaning. In this fashion man became a
captive of his subjectivity, the ego his prison. And from this prison
there was no escape. Each individual, according to his particular
way of experiencing self, made of himself a net in which the whole
cosmos was enmeshed.

One root of this ego-reference is the role of the Christian super-
person after removal from its spiritual frame of reference. The
thought of an ego enduring from eternity to eternity, after the
Christian notions of immortality and the hereafter had collapsed,
became an exaggerated notion of individuality. In existentialist
philosophy the old Judeo-Christian idea of God as the "altogether
other" was transformed into the philosophic-psychological thesis
that the decisive human experience is a confrontation of the "altogether other" by the lonely transcendent ego. The eternal person,
in this concept, in its mundane character is bound in a strait jacket

from which there is no release. Once the individual ego has been robbed of the hope of release in the hereafter and man is no longer able to believe in any way that he can be quit of the tensions of his individuality, the ego begins to flit like a ghost through history, always trying to come to terms with its destiny, while at the same time making this search the central event of cosmic experience.

Existentialism is a philosophy born of Christian despair, a way of thinking that has retained Christian metapsychology while abandoning Christian metaphysics. The feeling of anxiety and lostness that is the mark of this philosophy is rooted in the fear of the secularized Christian of never being released from his subjectivity. Thus arises the alternative between an heroic nihilism, which affirms this fate, and a sentimental positivism which flees from it and which yearns to rediscover the secure refuge of the Christian notion of the world.

The literary subjectivist movement at the beginning developed independently of the philosophical movement, though at a later date the two have repeatedly merged. The passion of thought shown by European man at the beginning of the past century when he rushed to explore the abysses of his own nature—the blind and burning love with which he ventured out upon the perilous oceans of the soul—these were not the result of scientific or philosophic discovery, but the fruit of literary effort. Literature is the mother of psychology and psychologism, for its real object has always been the individual. And in his analyses the poet often stumbles upon yawning deeps.

Just about the time when the aging privy counselor, Goethe, saw himself obliged, in view of certain deeply repugnant tendencies in contemporary writing, to avow that he, thank heavens, did not really know himself nor have any desire to do so—at this juncture man in his humanity was being discovered by poets of the romantic and psychological schools. Fascinated by the drama of inward-ness, the new literature, as it anatomized, broke the ego down into countless strange elements, all of which seemed to be held together by a definite lawfulness. And the very core of the human person, the real *principium individuationis*, stood revealed as specifically subject to causality, an automaton functioning thus and so of necessity. Though the first writers and psychologists were quite unaware of what was about to happen, the discovery of man in depth ended in a complete debunking of the spiritually static theory of the soul, which earlier had claimed a divine and cosmically derivative character for the essence of human nature and affirmed its independence from animality. God and man's immortal soul simultaneously were shorn of credibility. It now appeared that man was in fact a creature hounded by his instinctual drives and his visions. His potential was spent in merely living out his own nature, and his life's task was no more and no less than this driven-ness.

Psychoanalysis and scientific psychology later tabulated and for-mulated what literature had been proclaiming for almost a century: the fact that man is a fragile mechanism of an obscure and driven nature. Everything hitherto encoded in divine mystification now stood revealed as so much idealizing self-delusion, a falseness that could not only be got rid of, but which had to be got rid of for truth's sake. Man had become a process, the nature and course of which were biologically, psychologically and intellectually condi-tioned. A very complicated and difficult process it was, to be sure, but nonetheless a process, a functional relationship operating in strict accordance with the lawfulness of its motive powers.

Since at this time the Western World was entering into the technological age, and so into the age of the rotary and other machines, literature and psychology now made a triumphal entry with romantic, soul-searching works reflecting technical preoccupations. Now not only a small circle of educated people and literary sophisticates, but everyone whatsoever striving for edification and understanding suddenly began to see himself and think of himself in terms utterly different from those offered by the classic image of man. And he was forced to admit that the new image of man was indeed a striking likeness. In this newly painted landscape of the soul he recognized moods and seekings he had only fleetingly glimpsed, but never consciously known before. Man as he "really was" had finally been discovered. But then, after the very base and deepest fundament of his nature had become known, the new student of the soul projected his findings, the structure and content of this essentiality, into the whole of the universe. Thus subjectivism became an ersatz religion. The romantic-psychologistic image of man became a generalized model, in terms of which a certain dominant type of Western intellectual tried to interpret and configurate all life whatsoever.

Both the god-fearing Christian's image of man and that of the enlightened humanist were models which, in their ideality, went far beyond inadequate human nature, and so doing filled a pedagogic function. However, the new idea of man, as a being indifferently condemned to both good and evil, was not a paradigm, but a simple, true-to-life representation of operative human nature. It provided no means of gaining mastery over the as-yet-not-human. On the contrary, it tended to lead ever deeper down into the inhuman and subhuman. Compared with this kind of thinking, even rationalism was idealistic. For rationalism, in its unshakeable belief in man's cognitive nature, paid such homage to man's knowing and ordering power as to look quite beyond his merely factual capacities. In this sense, certainly, rationalism was a humanizing influence where the romantic idea of man was not.

With the coming of the romantic, the model of man as a creature striving for justice, virtue and self-conquest lost its force and was replaced by a literal image of man caught in the toils of his all too human shortcomings. Upon the romantic's advent, the humanistic ideal seemed to have something boresome and superficial about it. In its new guise the concept of "humanity" began to have a changing, opalescent character, an ambivalence which made it hard to tell whether humanity or animality was intended. The Middle Ages burned witches in the conviction (or on the pretext) that these females were possessed by evil spirits, though these spirits could be exorcised. But now it appeared that man was possessed in his own private and deepest nature. Passion and depravity were not alien to him at all, something that entered into him from the outside. They were, rather, a content and characteristic normal to his makeup.

Once this kind of humanity came to have recognition, man began industriously to rummage about in the dark side of his nature. In primitive magic there is a principle, extant to this day in German folklore, which says "never paint the devil on the wall," since by so doing you invite his appearance. When Goethe created Werther a veritable Werther inflation ensued. Oedipus, whose fate the Greeks conceived as a nightmare almost surpassing belief, at the turn of this last century became a commonplace, used to explain away and justify hundreds of conflicts of all description.

Up to the romantic period, philosophy, as far as it was not theology's handmaid, had been based on ontology and cosmology; that is, it had been largely devoted to finding answers to questions concerning the substances and structures of the environment. After the romantic period philosophy became mainly concerned with theories of experience revolving about man himself. Poetry evolved into philosophy and philosophy into psychology. A speculatively poetic description of psychic events sublimated subjective tendencies as actually exerienced and lived out, into the very meaning of life itself.

The literature and art of any period bear unimpeachable witness to its general intellectual drift. In these areas of human activity the currently ruling image of the world and the dominant religious convictions are spontaneously and unequivocally revealed. In its operative aspect reality imposes certain limits on man and man's desires. As a thinking being dealing with this side of reality man designs theories and programs which, as often as not, tend more to veil and obscure than to clarify. It is art that provides man's truest self-portrait. And it is during periods of transition, when there are neither great deeds nor great conceptions, that the "spirit of the times" is most clearly expressed in works of art. In such epochs artistic production is distinguished by an unexampled richness of stylistic experiment.

The history of literature and painting has hardly ever witnessed such a profusion of experiments in form, such subtly artistic descriptions and soundings in depth, as those produced in the century from 1850 to 1950. The overwhelming majority of these works are expressions of an encapsulated sensibility and intellect, bereft in all respects of a comprehensive understanding of existence. In them we discern the same confusion in respect of emotional and intuitive insight into the nature of things as that found in the realm of reason among what might be called the scientific superstitions. The collapse of the whole superstructure of inherited religion forced art into the position of having to shoulder the metaphysical task. In so doing art's real concern, which is to awaken and foster man's sensitivity toward all being, suffered debasement and became involved in the business of creating dogmatic theories of subjective release. Works of art, as it were, became mere hieroglyphy, the artist a magician and the erstwhile connoisseur a mere adept. The

formal elements from which any work of art must be constructed
ceased to be thought of and used as means to describe what lay
behind them. Instead they were represented as containing whatever meaning might be at hand.

Playing with colors and forms as the expression of a highly developed artistic technique and a sophisticated taste is a characteristic
of art among all peoples and in all ages. However, the elevation of
esthetic potentialities to the rank of theory and ideology is pecu-
liarly characteristic of modern European art. The antinaturalistic
and spiritualistic tradition of the Christian West, released from
the bonds of belief, of necessity flowed into an egocentric and for-
malistic esthetic.

Estheticism fails to provide art's essence precisely at that point
where it fails the truth. Playing with form and style for their own
sake, the figurations of which exclusively reflect the artist's passing
mood, is a sign of artistic impotence. Moreover, as an attempt to
penetrate the surface of "mere reality" it is like driving a nail into
a plaster wall and repeatedly missing the supporting laths beneath.
A merely tasteful arrangement of line or color, or even of metaphors and poetic impressions, imparts no truth at all. At the best it
only demonstrates the artist's intelligence; at the worst, it shows
that the artist has nothing to say. What makes a poem a poem is
not the writer's talent for creating a rhythmic succession of striking
words, mysterious tropes and aphoristic fragments. It is, rather, the
ability to communicate something by words which is not in the
words, as such, themselves. But if the poet never sees this something, or is unable even to look for it, it can never be conjured into
view by any amount of literary manipulation, however skilled. It
is generally true in this regard that whenever the reader is perplexed, he is merely echoing the author's perplexity.

The most pretentious members of this school of perplexity are
well aware that the best way to conceal their inherent defects is

to convert these defects into theoretical postulates. They proclaim, accordingly, that the virtues of genius reside in choiceness of taste and originality of expression. History and the universe, for these chosen ones, are merely a stage, furnished with grandiose props, on which they can play themselves in a series of changing roles. Of prime consideration in this mummery are the exciting, the fantastic, the unusual, anything whatever able momentarily to fetter the attention. As for what is true and good, these do not count, for they are tiresome, bleak and make for flat equality. Ordinary mortals, in this view, become the mere material of world history, mere spear-carriers in the *theatrum mundi* where the real, great drama is played out. The absolute esthetes here pre-empt not only the roles of author and stage-manager, but fancy themselves alone qualified to appreciate the drama as well. This theater of their imagination they mistakenly fancy to be the world, since both on stage and in the audience they encounter nothing but their own shadows.

Art for art's sake is a thesis obviously invented by people who believe that however dubious the subject matter may be, all one has to do is formulate it with an air of decision and ingenuousness and immediately it becomes information of flabbergasting importance. But it is senseless when an artist claims he has painted a picture which needs no one to view it, not even someone to whom it might have something to say. It is as stupid as if a man who had built a boat only to have it sink at first trial contended that it really didn't matter, since he was interested only in realizing the idea of a boat in the first place. A work of art sufficient only unto itself is not in fact a true work of art, but its mere dummy and empty form. Any true work of art is a communication, directed toward others. Through form a content is contained, with surfaces and foreground and background elements combined in such fashion as to bring to light a meaning that would otherwise be concealed from sight. This is art's real goal, to communicate meaning, and any esthetic approach to this goal may or may not hit the mark.

It is an untenable prejudice, of course, to believe that certain styles are *eo ipso* productive of art, whereas others, *eo ipso*, are not. Actually the old schools of European painting produced a great number of purely decorative pictures, as has the modern, non-objective school. But what has led the non-objective school of painting, and related experiments in other arts, to become such a source of vexation is solely the fact that the modern school has made style the basic issue and raised to the status of dogma the admitted possibility of painting without dependence on nature. Moreover, non-objective painting, in cold truth, is imitative of nature, for there is not one of its colors, lines or surfaces that cannot be found in nature. It is only that most people are simply not aware of nature's endless plenitude of color and form. Actually objective reality has many varied levels, each able to provide the artist with material. And what distinguishes the work of a real artist from that of a dilettante is not the source of his material or his particular style, but his ability to express the "*an und für sich*"—the "in and for itself"—in all its essentiality and idiosyncrasy, to bring a deeper and hidden truth within grasp by means of a composition of tones, colors or words. The world is a kind of envelope, a covering. But this covering, bear in mind, covers something. The representation of this "something" is what makes art of art. And this essentiality can never be revealed by mere artistry or elegance.

Whenever we lose sight of the fact that reality is more than that which we can grasp either rationally or emotionally, the fullness of the world turns into an hallucinatory arsenal of facts and figures, in which man sees nothing but himself trapped in his subjectivity. The uninhibited translation of intrahuman processes into art is a sign that the ego has been made into a universal measuring stick.

9

SIMPLICITY OF REASON

AND ARTISTRY OF THE SPIRIT

WE DO OUR THINKING on two different levels. On the one hand our mind is able to connect in space and time whatever factual content may be at hand. On the other it can create a world of imaginary figures, ideas and values quite independent of experience and then treat them as so much factual content. Imaginative thinking and inferring is characteristic of the early phase of all intellectual development, whereas an objective understanding of the world presupposes a great many and varied experiences. We have seen how Judeo-Christian thought took a purely intellectual and speculative direction. On the one hand it emptied mythical ideas of their natural experiential content and then used them as if they were realities, while on the other it set up Biblical statements as self-evident truths. At the beginning, then, is the word, the creation of the world through name-giving and conceptual definition. A belief in the magic power of imagination and abstraction is at the

root of Western intellectualism. And until the scientific period
came along the authority of the imagination in this traditional
sense was never seriously questioned. Mind in this free stage is not
oriented in terms of objective experience, or at any rate not pre-
dominantly, but creates out of the fullness of the thinkable. Not,
however, until the advent of sober, unpartisan, systematic investigation does the structure of reality as something independent of
man's ideas come to light, a structure that must not only be per-
ceived, but clearly recognized for what it is if man is to orient
himself in, and make himself master of, the world. When this
experience occurs, contact between man and the world takes on a
completely different aspect. To be sure, purely speculative thought-
structures are still projected, and an attempt is made to fit the
given facts into them. But more and more the thinking process
becomes preoccupied with things in themselves and with the business of making theory-building dependent on whatever footing
may be offered by real experience and definitive cognitive material.
For a time both tendencies, the one dominantly imaginative and
the other controlled by objective experience, can coexist in relative peace. But open conflict is bound to arise eventually between
the imaginative and the empiric schools. This occurs when the
devotees of reason begin to construct theories of comprehensive
application drawn from the data of physics, chemistry, astronomy,
biology and anthropology—theories which, in short, have an ideological character, systems reaching beyond specific data and so
clashing with already existent speculative world-designs.

In this conflict, which is not, incidentally, limited to purely religious questions, both sides have weighty arguments at their dis-
posal. Those dedicated to experiential fact believe they have proved
that free-wheeling intellectuality is misleading, dangerous and
useless. Those who place their trust solely in the creative imagina-

tion point in contempt to the triviality of the merely rational. The champions of practical reason are reluctant to accord any validity to speculations that can neither be proved nor controlled. The other side boggles at according anything more than an immediate and pragmatic value to the mountains of material accumulated through factual scientific research. The believers in fact point to the sensibleness, intelligibility, the general licitness and applicability of their kind of knowledge; the idea-believers play up the depth, fullness and general cultural and intellectual validity of their insights.

The latter draw from imagination any sort of image or motive, concept or idea, as they choose; for example, the proposition that the ideal and the material are forever at odds. On this premise, the demonstrability of which never interests them in the least, they now proceed to interpret the whole of life and all its phenomena. They sketch out, let us say, an impressively dramatic and colorful picture of the history of mankind, seeing it as a continual warfare between the principle of light, identified with the spiritual and good, and the principle of darkness, identified with the material and evil. They explain life's changing circumstance, great or small, in terms of the suppression or release of spiritual tendencies. They do all in their power to support this explanation with a spate of logical argument, that is, argument which follows the laws of thought.

This last circumstance—the fact, namely, that once a premise has been accepted the ensuing train of thought can be presented logically and convincingly—makes it very hard to differentiate between real and merely supposititious modes of viewing. The intellectual history of the West is striking proof of the platitude that anything can be "proved." For the kind of intellect which has a penchant for abstract deduction there is no measuring stick to test the truth of what is laid down with such unabashed resolve. In this realm thinking and inferring, analyzing and proving, can become an affair of pure artistry. The thinker has a choice of looking at life from a monist or dualist, static or dynamic, esthetic, economic or sociological point of view. Presently, on the arbitrarily chosen foundation, a stately edifice of theory, claims and norms rises up into the air. The average brain has no choice but to accept this sleight-of-hand performance as plausible, at least until other, no less plausible conceptions and programs are oppositely invented. The intellect's ability to handle propositions logically, even though the whole argument may be built on sand, makes the speculative mind an unimaginably supple yet highly suspect instrument for the discovery of truth.

But since man draws motivations for his conduct from the realm of the ideal and is able to a remarkable degree to live contrary to his own nature and the nature of his environment, dreams and fictions are no less actively involved in shaping history than theories based on experience. In sum, the fictitious is effective as long as it is believed, or at any rate as long as it is deemed official by those who possess social power and intellectual authority.

However, the hegemony of the speculative spirit in the countries of the West was broken as it gradually became bruited about that the mere intellectual polish of a proposition was no guarantee of its verity, indeed, rather an occasion for skepticism. At the same time the very scope and opportunity for the uninhibited unfolding of imaginative ideas began visibly to shrink. Each new experiment and scientific discovery brought the light of objective knowledge to bear on hitherto only defectively or incompletely explored realms of being, and by the same token drove the bright motley of speculation and fantasy from the field.

In the course of the last hundred years the general consciousness, that is, the aggregate awareness of a very great number of people from all educational and social levels, became so filled with experimental fact that ideas of belief of contrary import simply became unacceptable. Even though this regrouping process is still concealed by conventional ideologies, today no point of view exists from which to speculate scientific fact out of existence, no political scheme to negate the results of legal, historical and sociological investigation, and no ethical system to contravene the body of anthropological knowledge.

The defensive position into which the "speculatives" have been forced gives rise to even greater feats of abstraction. In the end this now artificial exclusiveness becomes an attitude deliberately sought and cultivated. Esotericism, arrogance and all the other unhappy snobbistic traits of a certain kind of Western intellectualism make the gap between the "aristocratic" minority and the "plebeian" majority increasingly unbridgeable. While clever speculative analyses of the topical tower up to dizzy heights in books, magazines and *feuilletons,* the world goes its own way, according to reason or unreason as the case may be. A pseudo-elite foregather in airless space, and there lose contact with reality even as they strive "intellectually" to encompass it. Thus arises the problem of a society and culture without a genuine intellectual leadership. The separation of the subjectivist-intellectualist layer of leadership and the positivist-minded masses is accelerated by an additional circumstance. All the while the speculatives are busy the vast majority of the cultural group, because of their greatly diminished imprisonment within the idealistic educational tradition, in point of fact are embracing new ways of living and looking at things, at least in an obvious, forefront sense. Yet the "elite" continue busily to justify the old, out of pride, blindness or piety. The mass acceptance of the avant-garde aspect of new perspectives of thought without adequate guidance from those intellectually equipped to

lead has dangerous consequences. While the intellectuals are
losing touch with the drift of the times, while they are performing
fancy acrobatics on their idealistic trapeze, the despiritualization
of a now mass-determined civilization reaches a point where the
exclusively empiric tendency becomes dangerously potentiated.
Meanwhile all intellectualism becomes suspect as a useless and
charlatan preoccupation. In the end it shapes up as something
to be savagely attacked wherever encountered. In literature and
the arts, intellectualism comes to be condemned as "decadent"
deviation from what, in the meantime, has come to be considered
"healthy" and "realistic." In political programs pure intellectuality
gets to be viewed as sabotage of arrangements which alone can
promote the commonweal, and in the philosophical realm as
apostasy from the "true teaching." Whereas earlier the intellectual
imagined that his legitimacy depended solely on a purely ideational accomplishment, it now becomes the fashion for every
theoretician to declare allegiance to "reality" and to base his
authority and claim to recognition solely on scientific or pseudo-
scientific comportment.

We see, then, that the matter is not settled merely by demonstrat-
ing the untrustworthiness of the purely intellectual. The idealist's
suspicion that empirically fettered reason cannot grasp reality in
all its dimensions is actually justified. A world where we could
think and act only in terms of proven knowledge would be in-
tolerably flat and narrow. If this were the case the impoverishment
of life would lead, in the end, to a stupid materialism and positivism, the frequently glibly described horrors of which all intellectuals
gleefully use to profit their own ends. The radical empiricist is
forced not only to deny everything contrary to experience, but
everything that goes beyond it as well. Since he can see only
so far into reality and since he acknowledges reality only to the

extent that it is scientifically accessible, his energies are necessarily directed solely toward making life fit, once and for all and in all its realms, into the frame provided by accredited scientific fact. Thus existence comes to have no depth or future, for both these dimensions fade off into the darkness of the contingent and the merely possible, zones which the sophist mistakes as nonexistent because as yet unrealized.

Only that curiosity which consistently transcends the existing content of knowledge is able to break free from the chains with which reason has fettered itself, to its own registered version of reality. Only by virture of this endless curiosity is it possible to measure human reality in all its dimensions, and by so doing enrich the world of that which already is, with the world of that which may sometime be. The transcendent function of the freely soaring, gliding spirit, which constantly passes beyond the borders of the securely given, very naturally entails the possibility of error. Nevertheless, it does attest the presence of freedom, and it is a prerequisite for that fullness of image whereby the creative imagination presses forward into realms as yet unexplored.

This creative fantasy not only anticipates the future, but, when correctly used, is actually one of the conditions necessary for realizing the future. If no one had ever thought of the airplane, despite all technical prerequisites none would have been built to this day. (And of course the reverse is also true, that the idea of an airplane would be quite useless without the scientific and technical conditions needed actually to build one.) The idea, therefore, not only anticipates future reality, but is itself a segment of becoming. It serves as a guide to the process of realization, it belongs to the reality of the thing it would bring into being. The unreal is that which has no existence as an idea in any man's mind, or which exists only as an idea and no more. Ideality seen

from this point of view is not the antithesis, but the beginning
of reality.

Man is not only what he "is"; quite as much, and even more
essentially, he is what he believes himself to be. His essence and his
existence are determined by mental images, imaginings, illusions
and fictions, ideas and ideals. The individual is not simply the
sum of his physical and psychic tendencies. He is the product of
these tendencies plus those intentions, or goals, generated by his
fantasy. Everything that he does is a compromise between that
which he is impelled to do by his psychophysical nature and that
which he is led to do by his fantasy. A man cowardly by nature
who—perhaps for this very reason—is fascinated by bravery, will
not invariably act in complete accordance with his pusillanimous
nature. On occasion he will correct and overcome his cowardice
in the direction of bravery. Herein lies the value of what we call
education: the establishing of a realm of values and ideal motives, which can be unquestioningly taken on faith and which
will remold man's "natural" proclivities. The history of the individual represents the interplay of given instinct and acquired
motive, of reality and ideality. The innate individual character will
prevail or suffer change according to the kind and the strength
of the images by which it is specifically dominated.

Things which exist and occur only in our thinking of them
are not merely nebulous signs written in empty space, but essential
and component parts of human reality. The way we live, reacting
and adjusting to, or mastering, the environment—all this activity
is determined and guided by things that are thought. Consciousness, as a consciousness of that which is, is also found in the prehuman world. Animals and plants also register reality, so as to
adjust to it. In human beings, however, consciousness becomes
mind and acquires the power of mentation, the creative ability

to reach beyond empiric reality and form an ideal world. It is only with the aid of imagination, of the power of ideation, of the ability to see more than is immediately present in reality that man can establish himself in a sphere which transcends precedent orders of being, a realm in which the laws of the ideal hold sway, not those of a material-mechanical or organic-biological nature.

Karl Marx saw a certain aspect of the relationship between idea and reality when he declared that being determines consciousness. This thesis is to the point, since all assumptions concerning the broad lines of social development must rest on an analysis of existing political, social, economic and general civilizational circumstance. The mind, in its ideal aspect, is able to anticipate tendencies as yet inchoate, but which will eventually determine the future. The concept of "being" must therefore be thought of as potential, and not as actualized, reality. In this general regard it would be interesting to compile a list of all historical interpretations and prognoses which time proved to be correct and another list proved to be wrong. This could be profitably done for the realm of political and cultural as well as for scientific development. Testing out such a compilation would reveal why this prophet failed to divine the future and why this other one hit the mark, and how and to what extent the human mind is able to prognosticate.

Tomorrow provides the criteria for the politics of today. Time bears out the foresighted statesman, for the reason that he has already taken the future into account. Time passes the political realist by, because he stands in time's way. Before he has got his treaty system safely established and can harvest the fruit of his labors, the circumstances on which his reckoning was based have long since ceased to exist. This is what happens to devotees of fact in the conservative area of politics. The conservative sticks ob-

stinately to the "tried and true." He is convinced that every
political program which hinges on future realities is an assault on
law and order. On the other hand, the statesman whose visions
of the future do not proceed out of given circumstance also comes
to grief. Dream castles by definition can never actually be built.
Forecasts can evolve fruitfully only out of given, concrete conditions. It is at this crossroads that the progressive politician parts
company with the utopian.

But how can we ever tell when ideational man is producing
ideas pregnant with the future or merely indulging in misleading
speculation? The criterion enabling us to distinguish between the
abortive and the fruitful idea turns out to be the idea's relation
to reason, its proportion of reasonableness. But "reason" in this
context must not be limited to the scientific grasp of existence. It
must also include all of man's opinions and intuitions as he faces
up to the world in an unprejudiced, sensible and critical fashion.
The legitimate field of use of the free imagination, the ideational
faculty, begins over and beyond realms already manifestly opened
up and staked out by reason. In other words, the things and relationships of reality which have already been grasped in their objective structure are no longer open to free speculation. "Free"
speculation! The facts on which psychoanalysis or Darwinism are
based naturally can suddenly assume a post-Freudian or post-
Darwinian aspect by virtue of fresh investigations. Nevertheless,
the discoveries relating to man's descent and the libido remain
constituent parts of knowledge, factors which every psychology
and biology, and in general every meaningful attempt whatsoever
to form a factually grounded view of life, must take into account.
Therefore, any intellectual flight which, out of blindness or hostility
to common sense, thinks of the mind's freedom as freedom arbitrarily to formulate questions about facts which, so it says, can

be illuminated "only" by the *ratio*, or reasoning faculty, forfeits the ability to think and plan correctly, and with this loses all claim to authority.

The history of the bitter struggle between Christian dogma and modern science is impressive evidence of the inevitable defeat of the spiritualistic cast of thought, and points up the fact that often an attempt is made to hold fast to a position by sheer force when actually it has long since been pre-empted by experience. The Church's condemnation of the Copernican theory, resulting from the trial of Galileo Galilei in 1616, was not retracted until 1835. But in time, observe, it was retracted. As soon as notions of belief begin clearly to run counter to experiential fact, more and more their power to persuade is lost and more and more they sink to the status of mere literature. They are either ignored, or among the pious are tacitly taken to be fables or metaphors, which may contain a "deeper sense," but in which no actuality resides.

Although unquestionably there are still a great number of people who take at face value the creation of the world in six days, the revealed character of the Bible, the filial divinity of the Nazarene and his being born of a virgin, the transubstantiation of bread and wine into the body and blood of Christ, etc., the majority today are kept from openly declaring these teachings to be incredible and unacceptable only out of fear of public reprisal. The Roman Catholic Church's resolute insistence on absurd tenets of belief and its fairly recent reaffirmation of its basic contempt for reason through the elevation to dogma of the Assumption of the Blessed Virgin, in fact signify neither victory nor affirmation for Christian spiritualism. In truth they signify retreat. A man sticks all the harder to his position when he feels the ground giving way beneath his feet.

Belief is necessary to pull man forward into a richer, better and still unknown future. Belief is also needed for us to achieve, out of our fragmentary knowledge, some intimation of reality as a whole. On the other hand, if we continue to play the purely ideational faculty off against reason, and to stand pat on the credibility of myths and ideologies grown obsolete, more and more are we left with nothing but facts. We then tend to lose our ability to accept anything at all outside the realm of immediate experience. A good photograph comes to mean more to us than any painting. We understand politics as conformity to current circumstance and our whole outlook on the world becomes restricted to what can be immediately conceived and calculated. The mendacity of a spiritualism grown arrogant and aggressive only serves to drive man into the stupidities of the banausic, the literalist, workshop view of the world. How can it be otherwise when the only goals offered man make no sense to him, when the ideals which are supposed to inspire him, and the desires and solutions which are commended to him, bear no correspondence at all to his own ideas?

Things about which we have definitive knowledge today have rendered obsolete many schemes of world explanation handed down from prescientific times. Nevertheless, the scope of the unexplored and the unknown is still as great as before. The possibilities of finding new meanings and new configurations for life remain as numerous as always for the creative mind. But this must be done through and beyond experience, not against it. Mind is more than reason. Yet the higher qualities of mind tend toward impotence and madness if they fail to recognize reason's authority. Setting the mind to work speculatively in defiance of all scientific truths shared by the general consciousness leads to a progressive discreditation of all pure mentation whatsoever, and restricts its effectiveness where it could be most appropriately used. The contra-rational spirit gets lost in dreamy arabesques of hallucination. On the other hand, reason without freely soaring imagination gets bottled up in superficial reality. Only imaginative reason or rationally grounded intellectuality is able to find a secure point of departure for ventures into the future and unknown.

However, all peace treaties, syntheses and forms of cooperation between reason and the spirit have enduring value only when we are aware of the differential characteristics of the combined elements. Whether they pull together in a stable and productive fashion depends on how appropriately the thesis and antithesis peculiar to each are aligned and brought together. Reason and imagination, or the mind in its speculative aspect, can get along together and unite to produce fruitful interpretations and figurations of life only when the thinker knows where reason's field of application ends and speculation's field of application begins.

The great revolution in thought that has been shaping up for the past 150 years and which we must consciously bring to fulfillment consists in a proper coordination of known and unknown, of present and future, real and ideal, visible and invisible, superficial and profound. The metaphysical is that which transcends the physical without contradiction. As we know, the attempt to force physics into the framework of an alleged theology proved to be a dismal failure. Meanwhile man's need for a total view of the world and reality is a real and vital need. In order to satisfy this need we must proceed from the certain to the possible. We must not, as hitherto, dispute the trustworthiness of the certain from the standpoint of what, in effect, is the highly improbable. It is quite wrong to assume that the quantum theory, or for that matter the catastrophic consequences of the rule of ersatz religions, have made the unbelievable somehow believable again. We must move on, not back. The sciences have provided knowledge with a firm foundation, even though we may no longer believe that science covers everything.

10

FROM PHYSICS TO METAPHYSICS

WHY, COME RIGHT down to it, is something something, rather than nothing? From what basic source is existence nourished? What are space and time? What is life? What is the meaning of birth, sickness and death? Whence does man come, and whither does he go? What meaning has man's presence in the world? Such questions as these mark the limits beyond which purely rational, objective knowledge cannot go. Since our experience of the world is bound to space and time, it cannot grasp that which transcends these categories. This can be most clearly apprehended simply by reflecting on the fact that we cannot concretely visualize either a finite or an infinite universe. Human experience teaches us that beyond every hedge always another garden lies. Yet the consequence of this experience would be infinity, a never-ending succession of beginning and end. This idea makes thought reel and turn away. The human capacity to conceive, in short, has a definite limit. Throughout all levels of existence there are zones which are as yet undeveloped, but in principle developable. But this relative "infinity" of the yet-to-be-explored does not mean that we shall sometime cross the limit described above.

A very different way of getting to the bottom of things—the meditative and intuitive method developed in Asia—may allow us to draw closer to the mystery of being than our highly developed discursive and rational technique of knowing does. It would appear that contemplation can reach into categories of being beyond the power of the *ratio* to grasp. But insights gained in this fashion, regrettably, can neither be formulated nor communicated. Actually Western experience in this area is so small that a final judgment on the value and validity of the contemplative approach is not possible. At an early period the anticontemplative thinking of Christianity barred off this avenue to knowledge, in such a way that the intellectual energies of Continental peoples have been concentrated almost exclusively on the rational insight.

However, leaving aside for a moment our inexperience in these matters, it must be said that all intuition has the disadvantage of uncontrollability. The possibilities of error become unlimited as soon as there is no critical consciousness to serve as a final court of appeal. And even if we choose to admit the possibility of developing a practical and objective method of meditation, still there will be a bound beyond which no one can go. Limitation is characteristic not only of our rationality, but of human insight in general. Unlimited, absolute knowledge would, so to speak, explode our personality. Individuality and limitedness are interchangeable concepts.

Anyone undertaking to deny the ineradicable limitedness of human insight would in effect succeed only in renouncing all claim to reason's ability to catch sight of its own bounds. Neither the Encyclopedists, nor Feuerbach or Haeckel, ever seriously assumed that the day would come when man would be able concretely to describe the "final things." The positivism of the 19th century, which in its way tried to storm the very gates of heaven, originated from the demagogically excessive, defensive reaction of Christian-Western spirituality, the defenders of which must have felt scientific claims to truth as an immediate threat. In any case, right or wrong, this imputation gave rise to the prejudice that devotion to the *ratio* betrays a narrow mentality. Even today anyone who dares take his stand on experience and on rational grounds can virtually count on being considered by idealists and spiritualists of all shades as lacking in true intellect and insight. At the same time the implication is got across that a really deeper and richer species of thinker can be recognized by the degree of contempt which he accords the *ratio*.

Nevertheless, there was and still is a naïve kind of rationalism which does incline to believe that the reduction to rational understanding of the whole plenum of reality in all its relationships is only a matter of time. And it is the windy apostrophes of this small sect, a splinter group never taken seriously by the true rationalists, on which all manner of Western antirationalists depend for critical exercise. The deduction at which the antirationalists arrive, in this connection, is just the opposite. They say that reality as thus far explored and as still to be explored by reason, compared with what we can never grasp, is so superficial, so trivial and dubious, that trying to get a picture of the true nature of things on such terms makes little or no sense. In the face of being's unfathomable depths, of the endlessly receding horizons of reality as it "really" is, rational human insight, together with everything that reason believes to have established as certain knowledge, is no more than a troubled dream. Our mundane criteria have no meaning. In themselves they tell us nothing. We register only sensations that we have already projected, and understanding extracts no more than content previously insinuated. Reason is not only an inadequate instrument. It provides no means or way at all to approach the truth.

Here different minds go different ways. Once a decision has been made to deny that the human cognitive capacity and all that it purportedly grasps of existence have no relation to truth and reality, then the way is thrown wide open to all sorts of world interpretation. It then is beside the point to worry about finding a correspondence between what is believed about "final things" and information brought to light scientifically. Indeed, the situation has then pretty nearly reached a pass where ideas of belief seem all the more true the more they contradict reason. Here belief is not cherished despite its absurdity, but because of it. However, if on the other hand a lingering conviction obtains that the human intellect, limited though it may be and capable of making only partial judgments, nonetheless within limits can still mediate an image of "reality," then certain creedal speculations become *a priori* excluded, namely, all those which run counter to experiential fact and rational argument. Here it is not a case of "not only, but also" but of "either, or." Our experience and knowledge offer us a choice. We can embrace, if we will, the fata morgana of a freely soaring, relationless and unmeaning world, in which ours is a phantom role, and wherein we can believe as we will. Or we can turn to a world—our world—which is merely one stratum buried within the cosmic structure. In the latter event the factual conditions of this world are at any rate elements of the cosmic design, and the limited segment of reality which we can apprehend at least does not contradict the nature of all reality.

For is it thinkable that what we see and comprehend of the world—though it be a most superficial contact—should be grounded in nothing? Is our image of the world an empty formula for an empty event? Or do inductive truths after all provide some sort of true image of being, clouded though it may be?

To this last question there can be only one answer, provided that the question of man's place in the cosmos has previously been posed and answered. Nobody can dispute that in some fashion and to some degree man must be related to the mysteries surrounding him on every side. Even though man had no immediate relation to God beyond being "made in his image," still man's essence and effectiveness would have to be taken seriously. For the very concept of being created in likeness expresses the fact that human existence represents concordance with being. It is a way of saying that being reaches into existence, that there is no contradiction between essence and existence, only a difference in degree of essentiality. The organs and categories whereby man is permitted to orient himself in existence are organs and categories for whose specific existence (Dasein) and characteristic being (Sosein) all being whatsoever (Sein) is responsible. We do not, in short, merely perceive ghostly figurations, but structures and phenomena evolved from the universal fundament (Weltgrund) itself. Our perceptual faculty permits us, to be sure, no more than a feeling out of the surface of things. But in and through this surface we glimpse a shimmer of truth. The whole truth can never be so constituted that partial truths cannot be synchronized with it, or its whole compass so scattered and discrete that the fragments visible to us cannot be fitted into the puzzle. If man is a crystallization and nodal intersect of cosmic processes, his intelligence must also be a medium and reflection of these greater realities. The truths of objective knowledge are in such event genuine testimonials of reality and as such provide a useful, indeed, an indispensable basis for all creedal truths.

Insofar as reason is knowledge of reason's own limitedness,

reason's awareness of itself, there is proof of the presence of a transcendental reality. Enlightenment and revelation are not required to arrive at this insight. In view of the fact, as proved by experience, that the rational field of action is limited, nothing is more certain than that there must still be something outside reason's range. Since reason—as reason and through reason—is reduced in observing the universe to the necessity of taking into account what it knows lies beyond its limits of perception, in this sense it grasps the whole of the universe. But this does not mean, once more to drive home the point, that in this grasping process the rationally inaccessible and transcendent can be concretely described.

In other words, so much is a certainty, and not a mere supposition, that only definite and limited aspects of reality are accessible to human experience. However, we do know that we ourselves are rooted in and interwoven with a greater, comprehensive reality. Our reality, in sum, is a part of all reality. Modern physics, as the first science, has measured its field of action and offered evidence that the unknown primeval basis of life is locked within matter, and is not located somewhere outside it. The physical laws permitting us objectively to investigate matter and put it to use— a process which meanwhile puts lawfulness to test—spring from matter's essential core, its final substrate. This by no means proves that being consists of two parts, one of which, the real and intrinsic, is hidden from our gaze, and the other accessible to us but separated irrevocably from its complement by an unbridgeable gap. Rather, it means that the accessible and inaccessible, the manifest and the concealed, are contained in each and every thing. What the dualists call supra- or antireality in truth is intrinsically real, an essential core as immanent in a stone as in a man.

The being out of which existence unfolds, that ground of life which eludes our apprehension, conditions what we call reality. It is precedent to and immanent within reality, but not apart from or opposed to it. When nuclear physics became aware that matter transforms into energy, that our scientific systems of coordinates register only symtoms and signs, but never the ground whence they come, the continuous relation of being and existence was established. Nuclear physics has progressed to that threshold point where being, out of an unknowable ground and according to its own inscrutable lawfulness, resolves itself into existence, to a point where existence endlessly slides back into the formless, absolute and identical, only to reappear as the formed, relative and specific, as the same and yet not the same. Nicholas of Cusa would surely have given a great deal to have his beliefs authenticated so concretely by this crumbling away of erstwhile antitheses. And the same no doubt would be true of Heraclitus, if he could have known that flow and movement are characteristic not only of rivers and the life of man, but of the very stones themselves, wherein the atoms dance.

Existence is being unfolded, materiality the side of immateriality turned toward our senses, the rational the understandable part of the irrational, space and time modifications of spacelessness and timelessness. The discoveries of the new physical sciences do not rob the scientific image of the world of its validity; they merely introduce necessary corrections, meanwhile generating an understanding of this image of the world as part and surface of an indiscernible universal substrate. The realities grasped by science are those substances and structures of "real" reality which have swum into reason's purview. The idea, meanwhile, that here there is a realm of physical events separate from another realm of metaphysical principles is quite untenable. The metaphysical is the core, root and source of the physical, and the physical the sole means of approach to the metaphysical.

To the extent that the term "metaphysical" indicates that there are things which transcend the physical and therewith our cognitive reach, a metaphysics can contain only those principles derivative from the panorama, the whole range, of objective experience. On this account it is improper to use "metaphysical" in connection with the free-floating speculations of a theology dealing with "other-worldly" events. These speculations, as we have seen, spring from a way of understanding the world lacking any relation to scientific explanation and natural philosophy. A metaphysics can develop meaningfully only when a physics is present. The so-called Christian metaphysic is intellectualized mythology, or perhaps a kind of religious metapoetry, which makes a system of positive pronouncements out of the fabrications of the human fantasy. Since objective natural phenomena can never be incorporated into such a system, they become, in this frame of reference, mere objects, or exemplifications, of the absolute. But the physical, in fact, is not merely material; it is also the medium of the metaphysical.

The world has no other-worldliness. Out of its own immanence the world's core unfolds, layer upon layer, form upon form of reality, a sea of potential and actual structures which come and go like ocean waves. The world is a universal continuum, an intermeshing process which builds up, only to break down, endless fields of reality in a vast metabolism. A recent astrophysical theory assumes that the universe "pulses." It suggests, in brief, contrary to somewhat earlier physical and mathematical findings, that the universe is not continuously expanding at an accelerated rate. Rather, after a stoppage and then a reversal of its explosive struggle to pull apart in all directions, it again draws together to a core and point of departure. This theory corresponds in amazing degree to ideas on the waxing and waning of the cosmos at least vaguely adumbrated in Greek and Germanic cosmology, and expressed with detailed precision in Indian thought. Throughout unimaginably long eons worlds unfold out of extensionless ur-matter, only in the end to subside whence they came. Each world-day is succeeded by a world-night, each annihilation by a rebirth.

Compared with this sublime cosmic conception the Biblical stories of creation and judgment day have a pipsqueak quality, like so many pretty little stories out of a child's picture book. However, even the most grandiose cosmology provides no answers to the "final questions." But at any rate in a view of this dimension the beginning and end of the universe, likewise the birth and death of our little planet and the genesis and extinction of human events, all run their course this side of the limits of our knowledge. Therefore, they can be described correctly and pertinently, that is, in correspondence with the results of scientific investigations of nature, or incorrectly, that is, in contradiction to all empiric experience and logical inference.

Every manifestation is a point of intersection and crystallization of countless causal sets and chains of motivation arising out of a common ground and interwoven in a common net of relationships. It is the essential identity, the unity in essence and the existential relationship—that is, the relationship immanent in and tying together differences—which lends validity and authority to human reason. The phenomena of existence as they unfold in space and time show their metaphysical identity through their physical interrelationship. Reason apprehends this circumstance in experience. It notes that all things are linked through cause and effect in time and space. There is no space without time and no time without space and no causality without both. Recognition of the thoroughgoing process-like nature of reality and the resolution of all elements and substances into fields of force shows the cosmos to be a universal continuum.

The same set of circumstances is indicated by the fact that, after having functioned in complete separation from each other for centuries, the various sciences are at last beginning to merge: physics and chemistry, chemistry and biology, biology and anthropology. The proposition that "everything flows" has become a scientific commonplace. Reality is a confusing net of relationships and processes, a dynamic building up and breaking down of structures ceaselessly arising out of and sinking back into the sea of being. As soon as being becomes existence, it takes on the form of a fixed system of relationships, the nature of which can be rationally grasped and formulated. However, the full depth and extension of being cannot be apprehended. Yet so far as we do apprehend this existential system, recognition takes the form of a kind of step forward, an advance toward reality, encouraged by the very flow of things. Man finds himself vis à vis reality in the same position as a child confronted with the problem of putting countless variform jigsaw pieces together into a puzzle of shape unknown to him. This task he accomplishes by taking the pieces one at a time until he has found two that fit, and so on. The whole relationship he can only confirm, not produce or describe.

Reality's layered construction and the relationship of these strata is a condition, a sine qua non governing the very occurrence of "reality." If life did not evolve—one sphere, structure or gestalt out of another—there would be no reality. A world that occurred as so many radically separated strata or processes would be unreal, since from one stratum none other could be glimpsed. Existence consists of a contiguity of substances and forms, none of which singly has any awareness of being caught up in all the others. Only the unity in origin and essence, and the relationship in space and time, yields an effective togetherness, that is, yields the "world" and "life."

If the psyche were something as mysterious as pure soul is
claimed to be, that is, capable of existence independently of all
other phenomena, or if mind were pure mind, then not only
would they not influence the material world, but they would not
even be able to perceive it. The fact that human consciousness,
in point of fact, does see, grasp and form reality throughout all
the layers and substances of existence is evidence of its connection
with this hierarchization. Psyche and mind would not, as it were,
cling to the human body at all if they were isolated substances.
The psychic and all that is "soulful" are based on and conform with
the corporeal; the mind and all pertaining to it are based on and
conform with the whole psyche. Modern anthropology, the science
of man, is working out these relationships ever more precisely.
More valid evidence for life's unity can scarcely be adduced.

The fact that all forms and strata of existence are universally
and uninterruptedly correlated is temporally expressed in the
phenomenon of evolution. The law of evolution declares that
one form of life proceeds out of another precedent to it, meanwhile
acquiring new elements. Recognition of this fact was already prefigured in the ancient Greek philosophies, until suppressed for almost two thousand years by Christianity's static concept of the
world. Even in the creation myths the origin of the world is described as a succession of events, not as a simultaneity. Life begins
as a single event. Stars, amoebae and man do not suddenly appear
all at once and independently of each other. They arise in succession, one out of the other. Meanwhile science has produced all
imaginable proof for this world-unfolding process. Physical phenomena presume those of a cosmic or astrophysical nature, and
without chemical processes organic life would never have come
to be. Man would never have finally seen this planet, had he not
been preceded by fish, reptile, mammal and primate.

The evolutionary principle ensures the pervasive ambiguity of all existence. In nature never can we find static, unilayered, mono-causal structures. Always we encounter forms uniting the most diverse materials and tendencies. Biological life is never just biological, but in addition is physically and chemically determined. Similarly, man is never just psyche and mind, but always con-currently matter and vitality. In each successive and higher sphere of being a new ontological principle, one not immediately deriva-tive from precedent spheres, makes its appearance, but the materiality of the level in question remains the same as that of the lower levels. That is, levels of being can be transformed, but never completely segregated. Nature is thoroughly "incomplete," since its newer and higher tendencies are always involved in con-flict with lower coexisting ones. All productions on a higher level must recapitulate all precedent stages from the beginning of time. All the relatively more complex and refined forms of matter remain forever bound to more primitive ones. (Here we see the explana-tion for the "completeness" of the world of technique, of things made by man. For man's constructions at any given time are derivative from and supported by only one layer of life. This layer has been detached from life's total correlation and freed from the tension of becoming. But for this reason man-made things are also "dead.") The farther nature advances, the more diverse and conflicting are the tendencies which must be united and equili-brized. Even the "gods," if there were any, would be rooted, together with their divinity, in the human, the animal, the plantlike and the material. They would, in fact, be no more ex-clusively divine than man is exclusively human.

The specific laws of each new zone of being have the character of purposiveness, of striving toward goals. They do not have the character of static demands to be statically fulfilled once and for all. They indicate becomingness. Man can never more than approximate humanity, since with him he carries all the baggage of his prehumanity. However, these residual earlier levels do change character under the transforming influence of goal-seeking human nature. In sum, man is not animal plus soul plus mind, but an entity peculiar unto itself, a continuum in which all strata have suffered a humanizing transformation. It is precisely in this sense that we can speak of man's existence as having "meaning," namely, an urge not to submit to the inhuman and subhuman drives of his nature, but to humanize them. Man's history can be conceived as the history of his attempt to transform through the specifically human all the configurations assumed by existence hitherto on earth. In the history of evolution, at its current stage, man is the last and most sublime product of creation. His downward connection, then, does not threaten the pre-eminence of his mind, but does limit his autonomy. The human mind can operate only through the medium of psyche and soma, and within their limits. The tension-fraught multilayeredness of human nature and the task which it must perform of humanizing all prehuman strata of being inseparable from it, constitute the human problem.

Anyone, however, who sees nothing but this problem must despair of man, either cynically or fatalistically. And anyone who looks away from it will only be ensnared by hopes that can never be fulfilled.

Human fate as a "tragic" thing is an idea shared by both the world of antiquity and the West. A feeling for the "tragic" presumes a stage of individuation found only among peoples of a specifically intellectual civilization. Man trapped within the processes of nature suffers, but does not carry out every twist and turn of consciousness engendered by heroic self-pity. Despite their high cultural level the peoples of east Asia have scarcely any feeling for or concept of the tragic. This circumstance is tied in with their completely different relation to individuality. The "I" of which the man of the West makes so much, as the Asian thinks of it is not the true and real core of self. For the Asian can peel away, as so many onion layers, the material, psychic and mental processes which go to make up the ego, the "I," and thus escape the whole problem of individuation. It is illuminating in this regard to understand the "self" as the concrete rootedness of our consciousness in being, that is, as the direct connection of all things to the ground of existence beneath the horizontal causal nexus. From this standpoint all sufferings which the "I" must endure have the character of no more than peripheral and foreground events, which do not touch the "self." This view admits the insolubility of human conflicts, but the insolubility now appears merely unavoidable, not "tragic."

It is possible to imagine that the fetters of individual character can be loosened by certain metapsychological techniques. But in our opinion man is not helped by such cosmic contact. He can momentarily withdraw from life, but he cannot live permanently in this state nor can he exert positive control over his life in it. To be sure, we have no doubt that self-contemplation intelligently practiced, like the comparable practice of psychoanalysis, can indirectly do good in this life. But man as a creature of action is inextricably caught up in the processes and conflicts of existence. Were this not so, it would be impossible to act effectively at all, or even to give names to what we apprehend. When man strips down the "I" and abandons his individuality, eventually not only all activity, but consciousness itself, disappears. There is nothing more to "know" or "do" under such circumstances. Existence has then reverted to essence, and the awareness of existence into being.

11

THE THREE PILLARS OF UNREASON

THE ARTICLES OF faith which affirm man's immortality, his freedom of will and the existence of a personal God can be called the three pillars of unreason. These three doctrinal tenets are shared by and unite all religious, philosophical and ethical systems which have developed in accordance with the Christian-Western tradition of thought. (Though, needless to say, they reveal nothing about the actual views of the various kinds of Christian communicants in the West.) If asked to comment on these three postulates the average man of our times, if he were both intelligent and someone of good will, would very likely say: "To tell you the truth, you've got me there. I've never really given the matter much thought . . ." And he might add: "When you get right down to it, all this business about God and judgment day seems pretty farfetched to me. But of course you never can tell. There may be something to it after all."

The subject of our quiz, in short, may feel that discreet evasion is preferable to open renunciation. There can be no doubt that the

Christianity of most modern Christians is more or less based on this indeterminate maybe yes–maybe no attitude. How far this uncertainty can be reconciled with the doctrinal demands of the Christian church we are not prepared to say. However, we are well aware that a great many of these not entirely believing ones are very much disturbed about their spiritual situation. Meanwhile, for our part, we feel this state of affairs is not worth the effort of striving to remedy. We prefer to say plainly that we simply lack the capacity to believe in absurdities, that is, in ideas alleged to be direct pronouncements from God. Since no revelations have ever come our way, when it comes to the question of taking such propositions as true or probable, or as false or improbable, we can only fall back on the sincerity of our own feelings, experiences and judgments. Admittedly there are things "beyond" physics worthy of contemplation, even though conventional philosophy might not think so. But this does not indicate by any means that we should take this as an excuse for thinking of a metaphysics as an "antiphysics," or that doctrine must contradict all provable experience and rational analysis. We see no reason on such grounds for exempting the Christian metaphysic from critical examination. Christian doctrine consists of a body of affirmations like any other, and these affirmations we are required by social convention to believe. Therefore, we feel obliged to put them to test in terms of our sundry opinions and knowledge.

It is a very curious idea—if you stop to think of it—that somewhere in the universe, on Judgment Day billions of human beings from all parts of the earth and from the remotest reaches of time will be gathered together for the pronouncement of judgment. But there is no avoiding this idea. Either individual man is immortal and therefore subject to a judgment day, in which case generation upon generation of men, women and children who once lived must be reassembled from constituent parts long since decayed, and thus restored rise from the grave, or we can think of such an occurrence as highly improbable, in which case, of course, there would be no personal immortality. The objection we may now expect is that revealed truths surpass human understanding and must not be taken literally. Such admonitions do not hold water. If dogma does not approximately or substantially mean what it says, then it cannot claim to be such, and must be taken as merely oracular in nature. However, as matters stand, the claim that man is immortal and will be resurrected on judgment day as he looked and lived while on earth is an unmistakeably concrete pronouncement. We are expected to accord it more than a vague feeling of assent. It is supposed to be sanctioned by our understanding and imagination.

If a proposition such as "man is immortal" is revealed as improbable and unworthy of belief when thought through to the end, the fault lies with those who make such statements, or those who hold fast to them. A theology which is based on revelations and dogma is forced to play a dishonest game as soon as it runs up against arguments from those unprepared to bend to its doctrinal pretensions. This kind of theology puts demands on our imagination at once concrete and banal. It tries to avoid all discussion, at the same time garlanding what are actually extremely naïve and simple dogmatic statements with an array of fancy and subtle abstraction. The whole idea is to leave the impression that it is the critic and not the theologian who is simple, on the ground, really, that the critic speaks out clearly and simply, whereas the theologian uses much dialectic and fancy literary footwork. The element of hocuspocus in theology and theological philosophy as they defend themselves against the forces of enlightenment has existed for centuries. The tactic is to insinuate a feeling of inferiority into reason, in order as much as possible to prevent its effective use. And it will certainly be a long time yet before the fact is generally accepted that a proposition is not true merely because it purports to communicate some darkly arcane meaning, or because it is cleverly formulated, or because it contains absurdities. Theology is not a science, but a kind of poetizing, whose business it is to juggle unproved and unprovable speculations, all the while making believe that such speculations have the validity of chemical formulas.

There is no explanation under the sun why reason should be treated contemptuously in this sphere, or why theology should presume to intimidate it. As far as the tripartite theme of "God, free will and immortality" is concerned, reason has every right to make it abundantly clear that the facts of the case are not at all what Christians claim them to be. To the extent that theologians limit themselves to the description of events running their course in the realm of the supernatural, they can let their imagination run riot, as poets do. But when they start to extend their assertions to the realm of actual historical events here on earth, they are clearly overstepping the bounds of their competence. But they do in fact poach on scientific and historical preserves, and therefore they must stand up to counter-argument. Jesus Christ's appearance at the beginning of our era, and his life and works, is a legitimate subject for systematic study by historians, sociologists and anthropologists. The life and works of Jesus Christ are by no means restricted to theological exploration and definitive interpretation. On the other hand, such questions as how purgatorial fire is supplied and the exact date of judgment day can safely be left in the theologians' hands. Whenever theologians make statements regarding events of this world, evidence is called for, and the burden of proof lies with those who make dogmatic statements about them, not with those who dispute these statements. Our theologians quite overlook the ground rules of intellectual controversy when they withdraw to the heights pretending deeds of glory, whereas they are simply running off the field for fear of not winning the game.

Man does not issue forth from nothingness any more than he vanishes into nothingness after death. He is a link in a long chain of development which goes back to an act of primeval creation so remote as to be beyond our grasp, to that unfathomable moment when being was first resolved into existence, the point of beginning from which the chain has gone on and on, a continuance vanishing in the infinite. The individual's birth, life and death all take place within the flow of events consequent upon the world's birth. Everything that has been, is or will be was potentially contained in the first atom wherewith the history of existence began. Life is a process of unfolding and differentiation, proceeding out of a reservoir and provenance. As organic life comes into being, various different organisms appear through specialization of parts and substances. These new organisms reproduce themselves and a species has been established. It is by virtue of the tiniest of particles that these species escape individual annihilation and re-produce themselves in the whole of their nature.

Every man's birth, therefore, bears witness to the unity and correlation of the life process. Being born is an occurrence without the least trace of the strange or terrible. No one is seized with fear from dwelling on the fact that one day he should have emerged from the anonymity of his parents' bodies into conscious individuation. However, at the other end of the spectrum of life, most people dread the prospect of returning to the anonymity whence they came, which is understandable enough, unavoidable though it may be. In any case, every man, after an interval of remarkable brevity, returns to that condition in which, before birth, he had presumably spent an eternity. The same vital force which formed him out of the general and formless leads him inexorably back to the general and formless. Thus, it is only for those who remain behind that death is an occasion for sorrow and despair. And they can take consolation in the thought that the deceased has only a small head start.

The tension (*Spannung*) immanent in all life, which man experiences as an endlessly repeated unavailingness of his human efforts, culminates and is released in the phenomenon of organic death. Life as process leads to a building up of forms of existence, but with equal necessity it leads to their destruction as well. Life is force and form, movement and limitingness, all at once. As rampant vitality life destroys the very things it has built up as a configurative principle. This dialectic game is played in each new sphere of existence, always on a higher plane, until finally, in man, it appears as tension and potential between soul and mind, soma and psyche, the sentiently flowing organic and the static consciousness. The desire to become is coordinated with the urge to self-preservation, the impulse to spill out the self with the impulse to hold it in check. Every creature has a desire to let itself go, which is complemented by a will to retain the unique form in which it is embedded. If man were no more than so much resistance to the flow and release of all things, there would be neither suicides nor peaceful deaths. Actually a will to live and a willingness, as it were, to die are both operative, and either can prevail.

It is characteristic of the human consciousness to identify itself with its bearer in whatever transient gestalt this bearer may offer. Therefore, the destruction of the particular configuration is felt as a terrible and vexing thing, for, as we know, man is eliminated from existence as summarily as he was brought into it. Actually, of course, nothing is "eliminated" at all, for that which, over and above the sum of its constituent parts, makes an organism an organism is not an additional substance, but the mysterious correlation enfolding and holding together all members. "Aliveness" and "character" are both a function of the elements out of which the organic and the characteristic are made. When the current supplying a magnetic field is shut off, there is no more magnetic field, only a mere formless and unrelated mass of iron filings. The factor, similarly, that is lost when a human being dies is the specific imprint produced by the cooperative workings of his biological, psychological and intellectual tendencies, an imprint which in general is called "being alive." The belief that individuality resides in a soul which survives the death and decay of the body is just as unlikely as the assumption that some day the person will be resurrected in his entirety.

All life experience, in general and in particular, leaves no doubt that each individuality represents an inseparable unity, which, however, is a living and characteristic gestalt only so long as the parts going to make up this gestalt function in unison. No known experience, or any sort of reflection upon experience, supports the hypothesis that any part whatsoever of the human person can survive self-subsistently. By this we are not implying an identity of body, soul and mind. We simply mean that it is an indissoluble correlation which makes the transient person what he is. André Gide once wrote that what interested him about phosphorus was not phosphorus as such, but the light emanating from it, and the fact that he could not imagine this light except in the presence of phosphorus.

Contradicting the belief in the resurrection of the flesh, by which is meant not merely man's soul, but his entire physical person, is the fact that the process of becoming and passing away moves irresistibly forward in one direction, never to be reversed. This process never re-establishes structures once they have fallen to pieces. If we think of time as infinite, then it is reasonable to assume that, given the same conditions, life will repeatedly allow the regeneration of similar forms. However, experience teaches that in truth the same event never occurs twice. Indeed, the temporal process in which all phenomena occur makes it impossible for the same event to be repeated exactly. Phenomena accessible to thought do not exist outside of time, and within the temporal sequence each phenomenon is different and new.

If the resurrection of the individual—each individual being, by definition, different in character from each of the rest—were at all possible, this resurrection would be thinkable only in terms of the rebirth of these specifically diverse characters. The idea of a person disengaged from his character, his specificity, is meaningless. Either I shall be again, and be for all time, as I now am—whereupon I shall retain the attributes of my individuality throughout eternity —or I shall no longer be what I am now. In the latter event, even I myself would be unable to confirm my identity, that is, be conscious of being what I once was. If we are going to cherish hopes of seeing all our relatives, friends and acquaintances again, this prospect, very naturally, can please us only if we find all these people just as we knew them when they were alive. For if we imagined them as deleted of all the virtues and weaknesses we once knew, we would be left with nothing but unidentifiable ghosts, not the persons we knew before.

Personal, conscious life is always differentiated and therefore limited life. On this account it is always beyond the individual's power to grasp the totality of existence. By the same token it is the dissolution of our personality which releases us from our limitedness and guarantees the restoration of our lost universality. The solution of the world's enigma, so to speak, is immanent in the creative process, which of course would not be the case if we were condemned to spend eternity imprisoned in our human consciousness and individuality. The very premise for the immortality of what constitutes our essence is the peripheral and transitory character of the personality.

Of course the question always remains whether death releases man once and for all from the chain of individuation; that is, whether the ontological process is such that man arises directly out of being into existence only to fall directly and permanently back into being. The theory of metempsychosis, or the transmigration of souls, disputes this simple explanation. According to this theory, if the world is a universal process, and if nothing can ever be lost or deducted from this process, not only must inorganic substances become material for new forms of existence, but psychic and intellectual events must somehow and somewhere continue and culminate in some fashion after the death of the organism with which they had earlier been identified.

It is hard to imagine how the identity of a living thing can be preserved throughout countless births and deaths. However, even if we assume that not only the elements of existence are immortal, but also that specific existential unities last on beyond a single lifetime, still the resulting concept of immortality differs from the Christian idea. According to the outlook of metempsychosis, life continues after death not because there is a "hereafter," but because life is subject to the conditions of "here below," that is, the cyclical character of all phenomena. In this context, too, the continuation of personal existence is not a desirable and ideal situation, but the regrettable consequence of being caught fast in mortal madness and mortal greed to live. The goal of the truly awakened man is not to become eternal, but to extinguish his existence and ego-consciousness permanently when he dies.

The unacceptability of the Christian theory of immortality does not rest on the fact that it advances the idea that life cannot end with death. This supposition is perfectly plausible and justified. But what does rob the Christian notion of credibility is its speculation on the nature and course of life after death. The idea that the soul, as a sort of bundle of good and bad deeds, should wait, quite unchanged, for Judgment Day, that this judgment day should occur simultaneously and finally for all souls, and that all souls should be reunited with all bodies on this special occasion, contravenes the very factors of universality and continuity which might otherwise make it at least intelligible. If the existential elements which go to make up the individual continue after the death of the organism, they must be subject to development and change. Indeed, it is quite impossible to think meaningfully of life after death at all without bearing strictly in mind at all times that the principle of individuation and the law of becoming are inseparable.

We are frightened by death because our consciousness clings to its momentary, local being. It is very hard for Western man, on this account, to keep this consuming anxiety at arm's length and meet his demise with equanimity. For if he is not entirely at the mercy of self, he is certainly highly egocentric. As we look around today we observe that throughout almost all the Western World, man's attitude toward death leads him to live as if his personal activity were never to come to an end. This gives us the impression, on the one hand, that hardly anyone actually believes in the resurrection of the flesh, and on the other that Christian ideas in cold fact are simply not qualified seriously to reconcile mankind to death. The "I" which Christianity has raised to a super-dimension no longer truly believes in the promise of eternal life and recoils with a shudder from the end of personal existence as from a monstrous catastrophe. Meager residues of faith revealed in such typical reactions as "naturally you can't know exactly about such things" do not suffice to blunt the seriousness of the question. Therefore, the whole business of dying is suppressed as much and as long as possible, and this despite the fact that any man who looks away from life's brevity and the uncertainty of death's time of coming is leading a life both barbarous and futile.

Anyone who has had any experience at all of the attitude and behavior of non-Christian peoples need not be told that it is quite possible to live a full, balanced life in complete awareness that it will all end in the loss of the individuality. Death and the corruption of the grave are among the favorite subjects of east Asian meditation, whereas in one of the most important Christian newspapers of North America the word "death" is not even printed. It is understandable that in an early phase of intellectual development and in a situation where life cannot be lived long and to the full, a people might out of wishfulness project the individual unfolding of self into the hereafter. But from a mature and rational point of view, no idea could be more materialistic, positivist and all too sadly human than to believe man's redemption and fulfillment should consist of eternalizing his precious selfhood.

This false evaluation of the ego also springs from the dominant urge of Christian-Western metaphysic always to allow room for the freedom of the individual will. This can easily be demonstrated. Although not only the old Indian philosophers—to refer to them again—but many Western thinkers as well have pointed out that freedom of will is a meaningless problem, like squaring the circle, to this very day the idea is being mulled over in the hope of finding a fulcrum point to topple the whole corpus of enlightenment. The quantum theory in particular has resulted in a "quantum" theology, which claims to have found proof of the existence of absolute freedom in the unpredictability of microphysical events. The rumor is repeatedly propagated, and by some believed, like similar fairy-tales regarding the final refutation of the Darwinian theory.

The truth of the matter is, if intra-atomic events can be only statistically predicted and are not foreseeable in detail, this merely goes to show that with our present methods of investigation the conditions governing these events cannot, now or perhaps ever, be completely clarified. Measuring the behavior of single particles is impossible, except in terms of probability, since the presence of the measuring instruments and the very measuring process itself constantly distort the image of the process under measurement. But inferring from this that events are not causally bound makes as much sense as assuming that because sociology always speaks in terms of typical and general social behavior, and cannot make pronouncements about the actual behavior of single persons, therefore the individual members of society have an absolutely free will. Psychology shows, quite to the contrary, that human beings do not behave freely and an "atomic psychology" would reveal the same state of affairs in the case of protons and neutrons. The "unified field theory" which Einstein sought to prove and which Heisenberg apparently has validated, would make no sense if microphysical events were "free." When we say that an event is of a "random" nature, this merely means that so far we have been unable to predict it, or for some reason will not be able to do so. It does not, to repeat, invalidate causality. The uncertainty principle of the quantum theory is merely another way of looking at causality, as Heisenberg himself has clearly said.

We can say that it is "chance" when a tile falls from a roof on our head just as we happen to be passing by. But this apparent fortuitousness, in actual fact, is causally explicable in terms of the climatic and physical forces which loosened the tile and of the circumstances which occasioned our passage by the house at a particular point in space and time. Taking away the principle of causality from reality's correlatedness leads only to self-contradiction. Everything that dwells for a time in existence does so in relatedness and in a web of necessity. And that which we call "freedom," as Spinoza observed, is nothing but our insight into this necessity, that is, its reflection in our consciousness. Freedom of will, so-called, is a psychological phenomenon, and not a biological one at all. The synchronization of our consciousness with that tendency in our physical nature to commit itself upon provocation to some form of action, to participate kinetically, gives rise to a sensation of experiencing a decision made by the will. Since we are always conscious of a multitude of inward inclinations and possibilities of action, a growing fixation on any one of these possibilities gives the impression that a "free" choice is in process of being made.

The very word and concept "freedom" tends to give us a false impression of what freedom really is. The point is, the structure of a language reflects that understanding of the world in vogue during its formative period. And since we are insensibly guided in our thinking by available linguistic images and concepts, we must constantly bear in mind that they must be tested for current applicability. A characteristic feature of the Indo-Germanic languages is thinking in terms of states, conditions. Whereas we say "the waves," the Hopi Indian would say "the multiple waving that comes to pass." Obviously this is a more precise representation of reality. The same holds true for "freedom." It is not to be thought of as a condition, but as a "freeing oneself from" while simultaneously "binding oneself to" something else. In sum, here "freedom" represents a transfer of self-commitment. A man who follows a moral motive rather than an instinctual stimulus, because of the greater strength of his striving toward the human, releases himself from the causal connectedness of the animal level and binds himself to the "motivational" connectedness of the moral sphere. This act, which has the coloration of his particular character, he feels to be free, since at the moment when it occurs he is conscious of leaving the instinctual drive behind. Man behaves "freely," therefore, when he identifies himself with the level that makes him specifically human. Nevertheless, when he has done this his decisions are still bound by causality and motivation, that is, by the general lawfulness of the sphere from which causality and motivation now emanate. There is no invasion of necessity by freedom in this situation. Freedom as freedom from all bonds and obligations would be absolute lawlessness, something that can neither be found nor seriously desired. Wherever there is will, there is likewise constraint. Real freedom would be freedom *from* the will, not *of* the will.

Belief in the existence of a personal God also rests on the conviction that the human (as distinguished from the animal) aspect of the personality has an absolute value, and that in consequence of this absolute value the human aspect must possess an autonomy of will. For it is out of a combination of these ingredients that the nature of the Christian God is made. However, once God has existence in this context, an abyss opens up between earthly life and the hereafter, and the continuum of being and existence becomes transformed into an unbridgeable discontinuum. (In other words, metaphysical dualism is nothing more or less than the absolutizing of thought in closed, finished things and states. Reality, however, is a process, an all-inclusive, inextricably interlaced becoming. If such is the case, God can only be either the beginning or the end of the world-process, but never an essence existing apart from, or in contradiction to, this process.)

The idea of the human personality as a static, autonomous quantum not subject to the process of becoming is carried over to the highest being, into divinity, and from divinity reinterpreted back into man. But however carefully the theologians try to efface God's contours, there is nothing experienceable or believable in this concept of deity. Either God is a personal essence, analogous to the human person, or he is something that cannot, and therefore should not be, described. Theology cannot wriggle out of this dilemma by adducing such nonsense as "God naturally is not a kind of man in the moon." Nothing short of a real miracle, that is, a manifest suspension of deity's subjection to the natural law of causality, would be proof of the existence of the Christian God. But to date such miracles have been witnessed only by those who in the first place most want to believe in them. Everyone else unanimously agrees that in their experience the causal nexus has never once been broken, anywhere or at any time, and never can be broken. In the best of circumstances God must be thought of as a deity who, after having made the universe, was then forced to function according to the characteristic lawfulness which he had bestowed on it. There are, as a matter of fact, such notions of God, which represent compromises between reason and belief. But a persuasive explanation for God as an autonomous personality has yet to be invented.

This transference or projection to man's representation of the highest form of being of the relationship between *homo faber*, "man the maker of things," and that which he makes actually occurred at a period when man had not even begun to see into the true nature of this relationship. What to the naïve observer may seem to be an autonomous act of creation actually is an event bound up with both the doer and that which is being done. Everything that man undertakes to produce is essentially motivated, and governed as to mode and method, by the laws of the sphere in which he is functioning and of the material with which he is working. The apparently "free" relationship between the man who makes something and the thing made, in truth is an involved interplay of psychological, sociological and naturally lawful processes. This interplay, to be sure, can produce wonders. But these wonders are still far from miraculous. Even if we should infer the structure of the "final ground of existence" from the human structure, we would still only arrive at the conclusion that our final source of causality, as in man's case, can be conscious of what he has created. We still would not have that key mark of the monotheist deity—the power of voluntary decision.

The final source—whatever qualities derivative from our knowledge it may otherwise be assigned—can only be thought of as an ordering principle, standing in continuous relationship with whatever proceeds out of it, and therefore, by virtue of this link, bound up with the rest of the continuum. There is a theory according to which God is not the creator of the universe, but the end-product of the creative process. Life eventually will produce God. In this view man represents one developmental phase of deity. If the decorative curlicues of this notion are stripped away, all we have left is a conviction that existence is an emanation of being, with the unfolding process implying a tendency toward self-conscious mind.

And all pantheistic notions of belief are also no more than poetic transcriptions of the feeling that a mysterious ur-ground of being is consistently present as a substrate in all things. If all these representations of universality are lumped together as the idea of "God," they share the common feature of trying to return to an understanding of the natural world, but this without having first completely rid themselves of the anthropomorphic notions of belief peculiar to theism.

All Western philosophy and intellectual history is fraught with this struggle to effect a reconciliation between the traditional and the new, that is, in deviating from the doctrine of Christian revelation, to preserve at the very minimum the concept of some sort of God, even if the compromise may have neither sense nor substance. For anyone who retains the formula "God" in his vocabulary and who uses it on appropriate occasions can be assured of the general good will, even though what he may be proclaiming at the bottom is godless.

Using the term "Providence"—a favorite epithet, by the way, of Hitler and countless others—is a sure sign of a bad conscience. In this term we clearly see signs of a tug of war between the belief that there really might be some sort of personal supernatural power at work in the world and the idea that this power must in fact be impersonal and merely fateful in nature. In any event, this dishonest type of piety in great measure has unveiled, for the general consciousness, the discrepancy between genuinely European and Christian thought. What is in actual fact only a reverence for Christianity's historical significance (or perhaps a merely careless choice of terms) is meant to be understood—or misunderstood—as signifying association at least conventionally with the "God" idea. Nietzsche expressed the true situation with great provocation and pathos when he said, "God is dead." Actually, Continental philosophy, as far as it developed outside the range of Christian influence, had buried the Judeo-Christian idea of God, centuries before Nietzsche.

The metaphysical core of the Christian image of the world is a belief in a static personality. This leads to the enthronement of a personal God and dictates, in addition, the postulate of personal immortality, and thus in turn makes freedom of the individual will a central point of interest. This entire metapersonalism—as we have already noted in our analysis of the rise of Christianity—is the result of the acceptance of the anthropomorphic ideas of God and the hereafter by a powerfully structured intellectuality which has been able to build up such ideas into a completely rationalized theological system. Indeed, the whole speculative structure of the Christian doctrine rests on misunderstandings, subsequently raised to dogma, of a naïve interpretation of existence.

12

HUMANITY AS A NATURAL EVENT

AT REGULAR INTERVALS stories appear in the press seeking to create the impression that Darwin has "finally" been refuted and brought up to date, and that, as a result, the uniqueness and nonevolutionary nature of human existence postulated by Christianity has been proved. But in such stories there is not a shred of truth. The discovery, at the turn of the last century, of the spontaneous, saltatory nature of genetic variation seemingly did imply that Darwinism would have to be drastically revised. But, as it proved in fact, this discovery refuted neither the principle of selection nor the theory of evolution. The law of mutation merely affirms the fact that the development of existing species and the appearance of new species may depend on forces outside the normal environment, forces which evoke an immediate and sudden variation in the hereditary factors. Meanwhile it has been demonstrated that biological development in general originates in those same minimal variations cited by Darwin, also that seldom do gross mutations occur, and then, it would seem, only as the result of cosmic influence. More-

over, to the extent that gross mutations do occur, or can be
artificially induced, they give rise to deformities and therefore
do not constitute a biological advance. Against this general background, mutation theology plays much the same spurious role as
quantum theology. The people who exploit these ideas have not,
as they imagine, opened the door to release God's putatively free
will from its imprisonment in the general flux of being.

In regard to the question of line of descent, it still appears to hold
true that the anthropoid apes—gibbons, chimpanzees, orang-utans
and gorillas—share a common ancestor with man. However, basically it is quite meaningless to spend time determining at exactly
what point modern man's ancestors branched off in the line of
mammalian descent. The genealogical line of fish, reptile, mammal
and man still holds good. Also irrevocable is the fact that man did
not suddenly appear on earth one day, but rather resulted from an
evolutionary process that took millions of years to accomplish.
In the light of this fact it is of no importance to determine whether
it was, or was not, some particularly favorable set of circumstances
which made this evolution possible. The main point is, it did
occur.

In point of fact it is always "particularly favorable" circumstances which give rise to the formation of new species. For nature
is always awaiting the opportunity to evolve. It is probably correct
to say that the development of the human species could occur
only under such conditions as permitted man to evolve his special
abilities unmolested by natural catastrophe and other perils, as
suggested by the extremely ancient myths of a "paradise lost." But
all that this proves is that the appearance or nonappearance of
man on this earth hung on a very thin thread, and that he might
never have evolved at all had only one of the many conditions on
which his genesis and survival depended not been met. It is not

at all as if nature were striving, with sureness of purpose, toward man as a "final goal." Like all other organisms this final product of the evolutionary process was achieved only after countless experimental failures. One of these experiments, for instance, was Neanderthal man, from whom modern *homo sapiens*, as is commonly known, does not descend.

Meanwhile wiser heads in the camp of the spiritual no longer resist the theory of evolution. They now argue in this fashion: It may well be, they say, that man, insofar as he is an organism, does belong within the univeral biological network, but the soul is something peculiar to him alone. This soul must have been bestowed on him by God. It is the "soul" and the "spirit," they contend, that differentiate man from the anthropoid apes and ape-like men. According to this view, the genesis of man represents a kind of super-mutation, brought about personally by God, out of turn, as it were. This speculation differs from the original Christian theory of creation in its assumption that man was not immediately placed on earth full-fledged as man, together with the flowers, birds, fishes and mamals, but arose through the introduction of a soul into some creature already present. The only thing really worth remarking in this theory is that it reveals supranaturalism's line of retreat. In effect, supranaturalism attempts to incorporate the evolutionary theory into itself, being desperate to uproot its persuasive influence in the general consciousness.

Modern theology is making what might almost be called heroic efforts to accommodate itself to the very latest scientific discoveries. The atomic theory, the theory of relativity, the theory of evolution—a Procrustean effort is being made to force all these within a dogmatic structure that groans in every joint. Simple minds are hard put to it to understand why it never occurs to the people who invent these bold combinations to lay their meta-

physical prejudices aside at least once in a while and think their
way into the suprascientific implications of the given facts—facts
which, after all, they do recognize as valid. You might suppose
that anyone who accepted evolution and the Darwinian line of
descent as correct, in principle would be moved immediately to
test the credibility of the Adam and Eve story, and not—as is
actually the case—insist against all evidence that it is a true
account, and that no solution is possible except to crowd biological
theory and theological dogma incompatibly under the same um-
brella. However, those who, from the Christian point of view,
are "unbelievers," or at any rate "not-quite-believers," feel no com-
punction about abandoning a hypothesis invented two or three
thousand years ago if it happens to contradict all experience and
probability.

In modern anthropology there is a school of thought which goes
halfway with such attempts as those described above. According to
this school man's uniqueness is not biologically derivative. Man,
the story goes, is "basically" different from all other animals, including the anthropoid apes, however unmistakable the physiolog-
ical and morphological similarities may otherwise be. Man, according to this outlook, is a "sport" of nature.

But for that matter plants are basically different from stones and
all animals from plants. Indeed, what new species is not a sport
of nature? And any one of man's characteristics in particular, naturally enough, can be understood only in terms of all human characteristics, for the categorical novelty which differentiates man
from his ancestors is not simply an addition to his nature, but an
alteration effective throughout his whole structure. Therefore,
how is it possible to wrench one special human quality out of the
total correlation and say it is derivative, for example, from a chimpanzee? Also, the argument to which Spengler, for one, still clings

—that if man were "only" a creature of nature, he would never have become more than an intelligent predator—is similarly thread-bare. Actually a predator who is intelligent enough to make fire and practice agriculture hardly needs an extra characteristic to be more than a predator.

On the other hand, the fact that human attributes are not directly traceable to prehuman forms of existence does not mean that the factors making for humanity, regardless of whether they were occasioned by the mutation of a single organ, of a whole series of organs or by some combination of these events, cannot be *indirectly* traced back to prehuman sources. At the same time, because there is reason to believe that an arboreal life led first to the development of the fore extremities into grasping organs which eventually became hands, this evolution does not contribute, needless to say, to explaining the fact that man can now solve differential equations and write poetry. Analogues of this kind are only polemic and demagogic in nature. They are, indeed, supposed to expose the simplicity of those who believe in science to an astonished public gaze. Between the stage when the hand and an upright gait evolved, and that of algebraic or poetic activity, lies an endless series of intermediate stages which only rarely can be reconstructed. This obscurity in no way contradicts the assumption that without the creature which once swung from tree to tree, and which later re-turned to the ground, there would never have been either a Newton or a Goethe. Formulations which explain man as a sort of "animal by default" tend to conceal the evolutionary past. They are intended to leave the impression that man is not all testicles and instinct, indeed, that his existence can be explained only through a miracle. But on the contrary, were man defective as a biological creature, he would never have achieved humanity. In sum, the idea that man is an imperfect animal is so much idealistic mystification.

Nor does playing around with the concept of "specialization" contribute much to the explanation of human existence. It is, in point of fact, the one-sided specialization which has always proved to be defective in the history of evolution, not those specific variants such as man which are capable of the highest possible degree of plasticity. The development of the hand, the eye and an upright gait beyond any doubt have figured centrally in the development of human intelligence, and it is utterly meaningless to call a creature equipped in such fashion for the struggle for existence a defective animal. Nor does this idea gain meaning by virtue of the fact that the development of hand, eye and intelligence was not limited to certain organs, but came as part of a "specialization" affecting man's whole constitution. All such constructs are secularized and conformist variants of Christian modernism, which confidently hands over man's body to biology in order to have a freer hand with his soul.

Actually the only basis for anthropology is biology, however little value the communal life of the ant and the reflexes of a chimpanzee may have in defining highly advanced human behavoir. In this regard, of importance are a number of general biological principles, a frame of reference within which all organic life unfolds. The ways and means by which the human intelligence determines man's life is a subject of investigation proper to anthropology and its specialized disciplines. However, the fact that intelligent human behavior does exist, and the way this intelligence came to be, are matters of general biological interest. The point is, the human ability to behave intelligently did not suddenly appear. It had to evolve on the basis of certain special zoological conditions, conditions of a general biological nature. Some of these extremely diverse prerequisites are the circulation of the blood, a general limitation to a single offspring at a time, a protraction of the period of embryonic gestation and an increase in the surface area of the brain. Out of the collective effect of these conditions human consciousness developed, with its ability to remember and to differentiate, to conceive and to communicate by speech.

It would be false thinking and formulation were we to say that nature has endowed man with intelligence in order to allow him to survive after death. It is nearer the truth to say that of the innumerable and random experiments which nature has undertaken in the course of evolving the human species, a certain combination of constitutional variations finally proved viable and enduring, instead of leading, as before, up a blind alley. Intelligence, or its precursor form, did not evolve because nature, so to speak, was actively seeking for some capability which would preserve an existing species of man from defeat in the struggle to survive. On the contrary, man came into existence after it turned out that this new faculty of intelligence was able to ensure the survival and preeminence among all other animal species of the creature in which it had made its appearance. Up to this point intelligence represents a chapter in zoology; thereafter, a chapter in anthropology. For henceforth the human power of orientation develops a life of its own, one that cannot be completely contained in zoological categories. The two great spheres of its unfolding are knowledge and deed, the ability to hold the environment at arm's length, to see relationships and to store up memories, and the power to withdraw from instinctually directed reactions and to act on the basis of rational aims and goals.

However, release from the realm of instinct does not mean that this new creature can act without cause or motive, that is, "freely." It means, rather, that the appearance of consciousness results in man's being able to put distance between himself and his immediate environment, that this objectification leads to reflection, and that in this fashion a whole sequence of motivations is set in train. The biological drives which all the while remain operative in man become overlaid and transformed by intellectual motivation.

Whereas the animal must be natural, man acts as he does because he "considers" his mode of behavior to be natural. This means his ability to observe himself forces him not merely to act, but to find an explanation for why he acts, and why he acts in a particular fashion. Man is constrained to find reasons. Freedom from the automatism of instinct occurs in accordance with an alternative commitment to the motivational nexus. After existence and consciousness separate in man, he develops a need and a mode of behavior peculiar to him alone, to interpret and to justify his own behavior, by assigning explanatory causes in meaningful correlation. But meanwhile, as we say, man continues to be guided by instinct and is subject to general biological drives which serve the purposes of self-preservation and procreation. The modes of behavior evolved by man, accordingly, like those of all creatures, have a natural appropriateness. Still, man knows what he is doing, and while so doing can imagine himself behaving differently. He discovers those forms of behavior more acceptable not only to the whole society in which he lives, but to other individual members of it. Through experience he learns that certain modes of behavior make life more comfortable and tolerable than would be the case if he lived as an animal.

It was, of course, a long road from the time when our very remotest prehistoric ancestors evolved rules of the game in order to make the best of their tribal life, to the kind of behavior that we call "civilized." However, humanity's roots are located in prehistoric tribal custom. The special rules to which man is subject are patterns taken from his instinctual nature. It is they which elevate animal passivity to human existence. At the same time the unequivocal, all-or-nothing instinctual reaction becomes an event repeatedly in need of conscious regulation in order to find expression in the desired manner and direction. When a man knows that he can either kill his enemy or take him prisoner, a conscious decision is necessary to inhibit the impulse to kill and follow the latter course. Primitive man, however, makes this kind of decision only when it has the character of an unconditional obligation. Since he still has no insight into the alternatives of the situation, he turns to the supernatural to find a motive for behavior that runs directly counter to his basic drives. His imagination now comes into play, the ability anticipated in dream experience to see things having no existence in reality, only in the mind.

The unconscious assurance of the instinctual reaction is replaced by the magic power of demons and gods. The mode of behavior required of him by life in the clan or tribe is elevated to divine precept, to regulation by taboo. If you do or do not do thus or thus, the gods will punish you, or members of the society of which you are a part will be forced to bring you to book, to avert the gods' wrath. On this level every religion is a speculative system, the images and concepts of which express the collective will to maintain a certain social order. The images and concepts of the supernatural drama in which man feels involved and bound are provided by fantasy, to which reason later adds a logically satisfactory interpretation for the whole performance. The religious superstructure, whatever it may be, must not only be imposing to view, but also plausible and consistent, in order to be believed.

The great variety of religious ideologies and modes of social behavior developed by man at different times and places is rooted in the fecundity of the human imagination. So amply does it supply visions and speculations that different sets of belief can develop from locality to locality, and new customs to accord with them.

Comparative ethnology and archeology during recent decades have collected rich material on this general subject.

The discovery of the multiplicity of religions and moralities, however, is not an accomplishment of ethnology alone. Indeed, it is common knowledge wherever different tribes, peoples and cultures have overlapped one another. Experiencing this multiplicity gives an initial jolt to belief in the primacy and general validity of one's own particular religious system. It is an eye-opening experience. If we bear in mind how widely knowledge of other customs has been disseminated among the peoples of the West since the introduction of compulsory schooling, of books printed for mass sale, of the movies, etc., we can hardly be surprised at the general feeling of relativism now prevailing in these matters. And when people begin to doubt the absolute validity of their own particular moral concepts, then belief in the meaning of all moral values whatsoever begins to totter. The revelation, too, that all religions, myths and ideologies are subjective and speculative in character also tends to undermine ethical systems coupled to belief.

The devaluation of a reigning morality is strengthened and completed by an event that is related to the crisis in belief, if not identical with it. People discover, in effect, that the morality demanded by the leading institutions and representatives of their society is still sanctioned by the powers that be, even though those subject to it are by virtue of this subjection rendered incapable of improving the social and other conditions of their existence. Customary standards become unworthy of belief when the people find out they are being imposed merely to justify the privileges of the ruling class. In the end society's moral system is undermined not only because the behavior of the ruling class gives it the lie, but also because men who live in an insecure and oppressive social situation find scant opportunity for ethical fulfillment. In the Western World

especially, under the influence of spiritualistic and idealistic thinking, the idea has been widely propagated that the real moral and
human elements in man's nature can be appealed to and developed
independently of man's physical, psychological and social condition.
At the worst this idea is pure subterfuge, at the best a delusion, for
not only poverty and want demoralize, but the mere knowledge of
belonging to a social group subject to discrimination. Even today
the political and social leaders of the West still do not clearly appreciate the extent to which the development of man's human
tendencies is encouraged or discouraged by economic, social and
workaday conditions. Refuge is taken, in this regard, in the comfortable hope that the prevailing morality can be improved by
mere exhortation to do good, by charitable deeds and, as a last
resort, by police measures. Up to a point this method works, provided that members of the society in question, whatever their
current status may be even though it is of the lowest, still think of
their lot as willed by God. In a democratic community, however,
any form of social discrimination or even economic distress does
damage to the individual self-consciousness, and in effect hinders
and diminishes the development of the impulse to be human.

Appealing to the individual to repent and mend his ways can
result in an effective humanitarian improvement only when it is
manifestly accompanied by a willingness to recognize and to satisfy
the same individual's claim to a share of the material and cultural
achievements of his times. Since we are used to feeling this claim
to be a human right, it cannot be fobbed off either by pastoral exhortation or charitable concessions. The way, for example, our
society is accustomed to remembering and taking care of its needy
members at Christmas time shows that its leaders have never
grasped or wanted to grasp the fact that although almsgiving can
momentarily alleviate need, in the long run it only serves to negate

and wreak injury on man's just claim to human dignity. This leads to such curious enterprises as the so-called Moral Rearmament Movement, which tries to make another Christian message and theory of redemption out of organized geniality and mass avowals of repentance, this in order to avoid social reform.

The humanist tradition which lends support to all modern European progressive movements—though to be sure it has been discredited by the various currents of counter-enlightenment of recent decades—has given rise nonetheless to an image of man which has become an inseparable element of the general consciousness. This humanist concept represents man as finding dignity in the free unfolding of his individual proclivities, and as being aware that desirable external conditions are required if he is to fulfill his potential. One of the most fateful mistakes of current political practice and programs is the failure adequately and willingly to take into account this state of the general consciousness. If men are going to be improved, the circumstances in which they grow up and exist must be such as to further the development of a harmonious person, one who can think and act on his own responsibility. And anyone who says that this consideration is superfluous or of secondary importance is either a propagandist for the continuance of existing abuses, or is in the grip of the deranged notion that a sort of soul-bird nests somewhere within the individual— one which needs only enough pedagogical and psychological wind blown under its wings for it to rise and flap free, another phoenix, from the ashes of mundane insignificance. The decisive importance of social conditions for character-building is shown, on the one hand, by the fact that men who want to live saintly lives abandon all social ties, and on the other by the fact that the political idea most deeply cherished by all men is a wish for justice and equality.

Man is not an abstract idea but a creature bearing a completely

concrete situative imprint. He lives in a definite environment which
has a definite influence on him. He does not, as effusive idealists
would have it, live in a realm of pure spirit. True enough, if man's
willpower and knowing-power are great enough, he can free himself to a high degree from outside influences. But this dispensation
is enjoyed by only a steadily dwindling minority, to whom judgments on the general situation do not apply. To a point that cannot be overestimated, the majority of people are a product of their
environment. But where modern man differs in essence from earlier
generations is in his feeling of being expressly dependent on external
circumstance. He knows himself to be environmentally bound. The
feeling today, as opposed to former times of naturally belonging
to the unchanging order of a certain landscape, people or social
estate, has been replaced by a life situation which man considers
tolerable only as long as he thinks it susceptible to change. He has
ceased to identify himself with the particular social stratum where
he happens to be. On the contrary, he is apt in great measure to
feel that merely belonging to this or that social situation imposes
no obligation at all to suffer impairment, on that account, of his
natural rights and needs. An industrialized mass society makes the
good things of life available to everyone. And if the distribution of
these good things of life does not occur, exclusion from their enjoyment leads to permanent dissatisfaction, or, to the extent the
have-nots are absolutely determined to become haves, to a frenetic
industriousness that is only coercively amenable to moral considerations.

To free man from his unrest and his lopsided striving after material goods, there must be a change in the system which gives rise
to this unease and materialistic behavior. This is a concrete political
task, which cannot be accomplished by any such substitutes as
appeals to the conscience, Care parcels or humanitarian organiza-

tions. Basically it stands to reason that in a society geared to the
marketplace the talent for improving material status should occupy
first place in the scale of values, and that in this society the man
who is intelligent and able and who can get things done, if not
always by quite honest methods, should be the highest type and
model of human being. A sweeping reform of the capitalistic economic system is a prerequisite, and an unavoidable prerequisite, if
contemporary man is to become susceptible to the moral teachings
and influences which would then naturally ensue. The great yearn-
ing for equality and justice does not spring from a lust for possessions and a soft life. It springs, rather, from a feeling that the world
can truly be called human only when secure and satisfactory conditions of life have been ensured, thus making it possible for every
personality to unfold and achieve "mortal man's highest happiness." The much cited "man's freedom to be himself" involves a
process which must be set in motion, in the extremely complex
system of relationships in which man is embedded, from the
periphery inward. Nothing less will bring about a thorough and
enduring change. Many of the complaints voiced by cultural critics
of our day concerning the dubious thinking and behavior of modern man in large measure stem from an inability or unwillingness
to recognize the importance of social and economic factors in
molding human conduct. To be sure, there is still room for appeals
to conscience, but exhortations of this kind have a false and hollow
ring unless at the same time all possible means are taken to free
the conscience from external restraints and threats.

When we move inward from the periphery of economic and
social conditions to the personal core of humanity, we pass through
another layer enclosing and conditioning the core. This is the aura
of the psychological, through which and by means of which private
and social experiences leave their imprint on man's character. In

this shell all unresolved conflicts are layered and stored. Psycho-analysis, which discovered and investigated the content of this layer, in this regard speaks of inhibitions. The early investigations of psychoanalysis were concerned with sexually conditioned child-hood experiences. These experiences are particularly important factors in character development, though they represent only a portion of the total number of incomplete experiences which man masters with the aid of his suppression technique. Under certain circumstances animals, too, experience conflict between two or more drives, say between the drives of sex and hunger. But should conflict arise on this level there is no suppression of the underlying impulse, since the moment that the animal yields to the dominant drive, the one conflicting with it ceases to exist. Therefore, we can use the term "suppression" or "inhibition" only if the inhibited drive is retained in the subconscious, there to unfold, uncontrolled, in a life of its own. In sum, there can be no suppression without the ability to store up memories, or without that specifically human characteristic which we have described as the compulsion to under-stand motives and to assign causes. A decision which is not con-sciously and freely made is not recognized by the human conscience, and so settles down in the subconscious memory as an unresolved conflict. This conflict is resolved only when its necessity is open to rational insight, or when it is felt to be the self-evident conse-quence of a command accepted without hesitation, as a matter of course.

Epidemics of suppression, therefore, are typical of periods during which people adjust and submit behaviorally to existing conven-tions while at the same time doubting the validity of these con-ventions. In this situation, prevailing conventions are felt to be either forms of coercion from which the coerced spontaneously seek to escape, or as forms of self-sacrificial obligation. In both instances man's relation with the world and with himself is seriously disturbed. People of a positive nature who have ceased to feel bound by convention develop exaggerated aggressions and extrovert behavior. The more submissive personality types are thrown out of joint by a feeling that life is bereft of everything beautiful and interesting.

When belief in the validity of inherited values is lost, new conflicts constantly arise between what one should do and what one actually does, or would like to do. Nothing less than insight into the genesis of these conflicts can resolve them, and this is exactly what psychoanalysis undertakes to provide. In brief, psychoanalysis tries to make belated repairs. But if conflicts of this nature are to be entirely prevented in the first place, decisions affecting private behavior must be congruent with the ideal human image in which the individual actually believes. A society, then, is morally secure when it is has an ideal human image in terms of which members of this society can orient themselves in a spirit of genuine conviction. Lacking this image, the human drive mechanism must be regulated without benefit of an established ordering schema.

Western man found himself in this situation as the Christian metaphysic lost its power to convince. At the same time the powerful influence of the drives in man's behavior was becoming a matter of common scientific knowledge, and this discovery, for a time, moved into a central position in the popular consciousness. Against this background it makes no sense to demand that Christian metaphysics and ethics be restored to save man from conflict, when those who make these demands have no idea how to revamp into unquestioned truths speculations which have lost all credibility. Fortunately, however, man's salvation does not depend on a return to theologically grounded principles. The discovery of man's subjugation to instinct can confound and frighten only those who had always fancied man to be in essence pure spirit.

If the Christian metaphysic must be abandoned from its foundation to its superstructure, the only choice remaining is to investigate man as he actually is. And this investigation brings to light the fact that although man is, indeed, a creature of instinct, he is not this exclusively or even essentially. Depth psychology did not, so to speak, hand man over to his drives, nor did it ever intend to do so. Rather, its aim has been to explain the mechanisms of psychic functioning, in order to develop an effective therapeutic technique. Psychoanalysis represents a decisive initial step in bringing innermost human nature under control. The general capacity to see objectively into structure and function implies the obligation to look into and establish mastery not only over the forces of man's environment, but over the forces working within him as well. To assume that exposing man's instinctual sphere is immoral, or that it may lead to immorality, is nothing but a demagogic attempt to discredit inquiry by diabolic association. For man simply does not study nature with any idea in mind of submitting to its laws. Rather, he studies nature in order to put its lawfulness to work in the task of humanizing the world.

If up to this point no one has succeeded in making the human drive mechanism broadly intelligible in this light, the blame must be primarily assigned to those who try to create the impression that the only way man can become master of his animality is to bow his neck to God's commands. But this procedure is out of the question, since the fantastic scenarios provided throughout the ages by the various mythologies and religions have not in themselves induced moral behavior in man, but rather have merely served to prop and justify moral behavior after the fact. First came man's need to act humanly in some way or other, that is, unlike the chimpanzees or ants. Not until this had happened was he driven to seek motives for such a mode of behavior.

The relation between religion and ethics is an ideological relation, an analysis of which reveals that the moral factor is immanent in human nature. Currently we find ourselves in a transitional phase between the collapse of a religion-based ethic and one derived from the nature of man himself. This transition is particularly critical because, as we have seen, the collapse of religious morality is being steadfastly represented as the collapse of all morality whatsoever, and is specifically interpreted as such by religious apologists for obvious reasons.

A system of "natural" morality will not, as a matter of fact, unconditionally or completely alter previous value systems. For these traditional value systems are themselves based on given human needs and strivings. Natural morality will slowly but surely approximate an accommodation with the rich variety of premises and definitions found in the older systems. For a natural morality is objective and universal in scope. Scientific thought guides the return of the moral consciousness to human existence itself, and thus progressively limits speculation's range. The concretization of our "religious" ideas and of our social and moral forms of behavior is all part and parcel of a single, over-all process. Believing only in what can be analytically understood of necessity leads to a value structure the standards of which are derived directly from the given nature of man and of things.

The objection that most people's reasoning power is far too inadequately developed to permit a moral system to be built on it, and that even those who are in a position to make rational judgments cannot act reasonably on this basis alone, fails to do justice to the real relation between morality and rationality. To the extent that this objection implies that human effort must forever fall short of the ideal, it is indeed confirmed by human behavior in all ages and under all systems of belief. But insofar as it attempts to promote the idea that mere intellectual insight into the appropriateness of this or that form of behavior does not necessarily lead to useful and moral action, it imputes to reason an ability and function which reason cannot have in any case. In respect of the building up of a natural morality, reason is no more than the factor which makes this morality intelligible to everybody. It does not, we repeat, originate this morality.

Passing mankind's history in review, we see immediately that whereas both reason and obedience to a system of belief have strengthened and tend to make perspicuous whatever element of humanity this history has contained, humanity as such can be evoked only by mankind's innate impulse to behave humanly. The average man has always been and continues to be guided by spontaneous reactions, which he attempts to realize even while adjusting to prevailing convention. If his instinctual apparatus did not contain a humanizing impulse, no mythos or lawgiving would ever have been able to move men to deeds running counter to their immediate existential interest.

It is also meaningless on the one hand to give man a certificate to the effect that zoological categories alone can never comprise his whole nature, while on the other to claim that the mysterious something which makes him human can suddenly disappear, leaving a chimpanzee or tiger in human form. Quite to the contrary, when man loses his humanity, he becomes an un-man, a monster, not an animal. Man is not an intelligent anthropoid, endowed on a loan basis by supernatural powers with the quality of moral grace. Rather, he is a creature in all respects different from other mammals, though not in the least removed from nature by this difference, but through nature characteristically evolved and by nature made intelligible. His specifically human tendencies are a component of the totality of his nature. He cannot rid himself of his humanity as a balloonist jettisons a sack of sand, or as an

outboard driver shuts off his motor. Evil is not evil because some
divine or social law has been broken, but because man's obligation
to his immanent humanity has been violated. Indeed, were this not
the case, there would be no good or bad at all, only licit and illicit
deeds. Goodness is congruence with the lawfulness peculiar to
human nature, and evil is incongruence.

The thesis that the contemplation of human nature is equivalent
to a regression toward the animal depends on an intellectual trick,
whereby, as the argument is prepared, the human element is arbitrarily torn from the whole context of man's nature. In short, this
thesis merely brings to light an error (or swindle) previously insinuated by sleight of hand. In point of fact the human factor is
part and parcel of man's biological organization. As such it forces
him to take an appropriately human direction even when he is
completely ignorant of his own make-up and still far from any
thought of conceptually differentiating between the animal and
the human aspects of his nature. Lacking the sure basis of a
humanizing mechanism, man could never make up his mind to
live a life worthy of a human being.

The presence of a humanizing impulse is expressed in spontaneous feelings of shame and pride. Here man becomes directly
aware of the congruence or incongruence of his behavior in respect
of nature, this quite without the intervention of rational insight or
of commitment to some code of belief. The theme of "man" is
generically operative in all human beings. This means that each
man finds in himself an image that guides his nature. This immanence is not contradicted by the fact that man is never able
completely to realize the generic idea. True enough, he does remain
bound to all prehuman levels. No matter, he knows very well that
his special quality must always be reckoned with. Expressing this
special quality is felt as pride, betraying it as shame. Man experi-

ences satisfaction in advancing the human, distress in failing
to do so.

Since initially man is able to understand the tendencies which
set him apart from the animals only as emanations of a divine will,
at this stage his experience of shame at having failed to live up to
the human takes the form of fear of punishment, and the pride of
human accomplishment the form of the hope of reward. Nevertheless, every ethos represents a posture deriving from human
nature, and is neither evidence of the workings of reason or expediency, nor a question of obedience to divine command. The
critical driving force in human behavior is man's naïve vanity, a
kind of self-regard which leads him to believe he can act selflessly
rather than selfishly, magnanimously rather than vengefully, fear-
lessly rather than fearfully. A man who fails to strive after these
human ideals sacrifices his self-esteem. In short, it is a natural and
human need for prestige which drives man to behave independently
of the rationally deliberated or the metaphysical obligation.

The average man of the West today, given over completely as he
is to the search for pleasure and to a surface existence, certainly
does not worry about ethical questions, or their possible rational or
transcendental foundation. However, the desire to be human can
still be detected in modern man. Even in the half-grown ne'er-do-
well, who shambles about with hands deep in his pockets, spitting
on the sidewalk in splendid rainbow arcs, there is still an instinct
for the human at work. He admires the young fellow who takes his
punishment in silence when he is beaten, and the man who ignores
money, danger or public opinion. His ideal image is the motorcycle
racer who risks his life to break a record, the explorer who, for
mere exploration's sake, dies trying to get to the North Pole. The
leader images produced by the films and comic strips, even in
criminal guise emphasize the heroic and the ideal. The sentimen-

tality or cynicism in this hero-worship arises from a conflict between an actuality shot through with social suppression, the obvious and the banal and an ideal filled with longing for the "beautiful" and "higher" life. Man's hunger for tales of heroism and
love springs not least from the need for vicarious identification
with the ideal human image, a perfection which his own limited
powers and actual life situation make it quite impossible to realize.
Man lives instinctively and spontaneously in terms of a leader
image in which he implicitly believes, an ideal in which self-seeking,
untruth and cowardice have been overcome.

The man who is not entirely naïve, but only half-naïve and half-
reflective, is in the danger spot. In this type of person the humanizing impulse can be attacked and destroyed. The half-naïve,
half-intellectual man is particularly subject to this calamity if he
interprets the collapse of religious ideology as a collapse of morality
and humanity as well, and if he is canvassed on this basis by popular tractarians who cannot see the harm they are causing. In this
dilemma man comes to regard his human strivings as meaningless,
and so suppresses them. If this does not make a criminal of him,
it will at any rate leave him lost, with no standards to fall back on.
Morality in our times on the whole is no worse than it ever has
been. Indeed, it is even possible to argue an advance in social
morality, a trend opposed to barbarous regressions otherwise experienced in the past half-century. The history of morality is the
history of a continuing refinement of man's immanent humanizing
need. Or, if you will, of his vanity. Man would not be able to give
his life up to someone else, to society, to an idea, if doing this did
not accord with his need for prestige.

A society, then, becomes truly human when it succeeds in linking
social prestige with individual human accomplishment. In this
sense the humanizing of man is very much the province of the

politician, the national economist, the social teacher, and not of the preacher of repentance and the writer of lead articles. Not until the highest social and economic levels of society honor moral, intellectual and generally cultural accomplishments and recognize as exemplars these ideals in place of "fitness in the struggle for existence," will it be possible to bring about a thorough humanization of the social structure. The pre-eminence of the human ideal, in sum, must be visibly and concretely, as well as verbally, recognized.

This entails the creation of credible leader images. And in a completely rationalized world these guiding images can be derived only from human nature itself. All speculative ethical systems are unworkable in an enlightened society, since members of such a society would be prepared to follow only those directions which correspond with their own convictions, experiences and feelings. Commands advance humanity only so long as the kind of existence and the authority which they proclaim are not eroded by doubt.

Today morality by command evokes resistance because modern man, at least as a civilized member of the middle class, has grown accustomed to thinking of himself as making decisions on the basis of his own, freely operating insight. Therefore, all moral systems which deny that a sound basis for human behavior is found in man himself, and which undertake to propagate the view that human behavior can be effectively induced only by transcendental regulation, are actually lending support to immorality. Moreover they are laying themselves open to the suspicion that they are more concerned with man's commitment to a certain religious creed than with his moral behavior. For practically anyone can be made to understand that man has to be human to be in accord with his own nature, but it is a shaky approach which would have man believe that he must be human because God wants him to be, and that eternal blessedness hangs therewith in the balance. (Besides, it is a morally less effective way of believing in any event, since this system hinges on the idea that man and God are, as it were, business partners, who keep accounts of claims on each other.)

Man, of course, can never expect to attain more than incomplete, approximate and unfinished results in his attempts to create a humanized world. But this incompleteness in no sense robs his striving toward humanity of sense and prospect. Whatever humanity may be realized at all in this world, is realizable through people and through simple human powers alone. There is no one else to whom the task can be relegated. We would have been spared all the tragic-heroic, sentimental-cynical immorality of the past century, had mankind only clearly recognized that humanity is a natural event.

It is not a return to religion that is needed to correct immorality, but a rational insight into human nature. Just as a believable metaphysics can arise only by way of physics, so must a believable ethic be built up on anthropology. It must not only be generally known that man is by nature human, but in what way he is human as well, if we are ever going to establish the necessary support for spontaneous strivings toward humanity. The humanizing impulse, true enough, can be furthered and given assurance through mythical and religious speculation, but this possibility ceases to exist once it has been discovered that such forms of support are merely speculative. Once this has come to pass, the bond between theology and morality is broken, since a religious ideology, whenever it suffers collapse tends at the same time to suffer destruction of its moral basis as well.

It is the masses who determine life today, and who will determine it tomorrow. This does not mean that the masses can take charge of their own fate unaided. But it does mean that the guiding images provided for them must accord with their world-feeling and their understanding of self. Henceforth accomplishments expected and goals offered must be comprehensible to the average man and acceptable to him as a matter of free and self-responsible choice. The new ethic will have to be a sober and sensible ethic, free from all rapture and extravagance. Nothing less than an appeal to the innate humanizing need for prestige, accompanied by an appeal to reason, can lead to viable moral standards and modes of behavior. Man must, in effect, be given the feeling that it is shameful to fail himself, and that on the other hand he has a right to be proud when able to lay claim to being a man among men.

13

THE DUTY TO BE UNHOLY AND UNWISE

THOUGH CHRISTIAN PEOPLES on the whole have probably been less barbarous than the peoples of non-Christian cultures, actually they are not too far behind in this respect. The total suffering inflicted by members of Western culture in their Christian capacity during the last two millennia in bloody wars and heretic persecutions very likely would not have been exceeded had Europe been non-Christian. And this is quite leaving aside crimes committed against the "heathen" throughout the world in Christianity's name. The claim that without Christianity life would have languished in moral degradation is completely lacking in conviction. If such were the case all peoples of non-Christian religious preferment would have remained wallowing in bestiality, and that this is not so there can be no question. That still extremely pubertal and labile state of mind characteristic of man about the time he appeared in recorded history, as all experience shows, can easily be reinduced. If proper measures are used to reawaken the instincts which mass psychologists study, man can be rapidly and thoroughly rebarbarized, in a Christian or any other society. In point of fact, under normal conditions man's private and social morality are much more advanced, and this advance much more deeply rooted, in the countries of east Asia than in the Western Hemisphere. The hardheartedness and callousness, the unscrupulous will to power, the inordinate urge to live better and better at any cost typical of Western man, these qualities are so crassly out of line with the fundamental ethic of Christianity that it would seem the Sermon on the Mount must surely have fallen on deaf ears.

Unless we are prepared to admit that the peoples who let themselves be converted to Christianity are by nature more impenitent and malignant than most, the only inference we have left is that Christian morality gets through to man only with great difficulty, if at all. In the Christian world, discrepancy reaches a pitch where there is conflict not merely between knowing and believing, but between doing and believing as well. And it is not a case here of ethical ideals of necessity being only approximately realized. The trouble is, Christian morality stems from an image of man in which the characteristically human mode of being is strikingly absent.

The Ten Commandments of Moses, to be sure, still accord with human nature in general. They represent rules of behavior closely tuned to a certain set of social conditions, and are reasonable and necessary within this special situation. But when we arrive at the lofty ethical summons of the Sermon on the Mount, we begin to see the workings of a rigorous and other-worldly spiritualism, impelled by a passionate need for conquest of all selfhood. Eventually, with Paul, a viewpoint takes shape whereby man must nail his nature to the cross in order to be pleasing in God's sight. This theory, however, comes hard up against not only the "all-too-human," but man's very humanity itself.

Confronting a human being with ethical ideals which do not

refine his naturalness but rather ascribe diabolism to it must in the end lead to resignation or to cynicism. This situation must become a carte-blanche for all kinds of surreptitious immorality. On this account a remarkable phenomenon has appeared characteristic of our culture: an enormously sensitive conscience accompanied by underdeveloped moral behavior in the practical sphere. The more dissatisfied man feels with Christianity's moral precepts, the more inflammable his conscience, and the more urgent his need at least programmatically to realize these precepts. The Christian-Paulinist morality has produced a culture in which the latest speaker on the program, as it were, has supplanted the original exemplars. In this culture the unattainability of the Christian ethical ideals permits even the most Christian of Christians to devise a highly pragmatic morality for their earthly dealings.

The Paulinist ethic is a theory of ideal human behavior completely in concordance with the Christian world-image. Viewed in terms of the end and goal of world history, this ethic prepares the creature, man, for his meeting with Christ and God, a consummation much more closely guaranteed by sickness, misery and suffering of all kinds than by a life lived as a human being under decent conditions. The instructions given to the Christian communities in the Pauline epistles have no sense at all of uplifting individual and collective morality for their own present sake. On the contrary, their intent is to get the community to measure up to the events and demands of the impending hereafter.

The most basic of all the ideas of Christian belief, the notion that earthly existence in itself has no meaning, but is no more than a preparatory testing ground for the eternal life, necessarily fails to lend support to man's personal and social sense of responsibility, and makes for blindness toward any factually oriented investigation of the possibilities offered by nature for solving life's problems.

Christians seek the conquest of the human, not its fulfillment. In this Christianity is diametrically opposed to the humanist concept, according to which mankind's task consists of an unremitting effort to preserve and advance the human factor. No "Christian humanism" can ever eliminate this conflict, for a religion that enjoins its adherents to spend here and now in expectation of then and there will never be able properly to appreciate man's given need to embrace life for its own sake. Christianity must also run counter to the human point of view, even Christian humanism, since the profession of Christianity of any hue involves a refusal to admit that man can get along without God and that he can see into things correctly and behave properly without divine aid. According to the orthodox Christian point of view, it is only through God's grace, on the basis of some decision beyond human knowing, that mundane affairs are occasionally allowed to take a turn for the good.

However, the fact that Western man, despite this unsettling influence, has still evidenced not only a strong scientific, but a strong humanitarian preoccupation as well, shows how little mankind's behavior is actually determined by strange and inexplicable credal speculation. Most impressive witness of this state of affairs, perhaps, is the history of medicine. The only possible interpretation of physical mishap and sickness in line with the Christian world-image is that such events are "acts of God," to which man has no choice but to resign himself. Yet at no time in history has this idea seriously kept the Continental peoples from trying to develop an art of medicine, this on the premise that every sickness must have a natural cause and that it is man's task to seek out these causes and eliminate them. Of course the Christian idea of sickness and healing has lingered on at Lourdes and other such miraculous centers, where cures are said to be wrought by bathing in wonder-working springs or by touching relics. The trials which God inflicts on man to remind him of his frailty and sinfulness, the Christian claims, can be taken away by God alone. But for enlightened man, quite the contrary, every sickness is a challenge to improve healing methods and the conditions of this life below. The Christian thesis later formulated during the retreat before the forces of enlightenment, namely, that the body can be left to the doctors and the biologists, if only the soul is preserved for God, is beyond any doubt a falsification of the dogma that man must be delivered up whole to God, and that whatever misfortunes may befall him must be understood not as a challenge to be met, but as an opportunity for the purification and strengthening of the sufferer's belief.

Christianity has produced as little thought in the biological sciences or for that matter even stimulated it, as it has produced methods leading to the understanding and control of the human soma and psyche. Both the world outside and man's inner world, says Christianity, are a welter of confusion and filth, and contain no truths. Whereas the natural sciences have broken through this taboo in the realm of Christian-Western culture, man as a medium of the metaphysical and metapsychic has remained terra incognita. Although man should be the one object of investigation able to provide direct information on the "true nature of things," for two thousand years antipsychological and antimeditative Christian theology has averted man's gaze from these aspects. None but the mystics have tried to explore these paths and they have penetrated no farther into the sphere of inward contemplation than was necessary to find what they were looking for, that is, the ur-images of Christianity's dreams and visions. And these excursions into the interior of the human continent have been frowned upon by the official Church, since they entailed the danger of making God, otherwise that superego enthroned outside the world, into an event of man's inner world.

For Christianity man is identified with his statically conceived character, that is, the ego level. The statically thought-of ego stands in opposition, across an abyss, to a static God, who can be approached only by a great leap of nature, an act of violence. In this situation religion has become synonymous with an abject readiness to accept God's claims, and morality with a willingness to do precisely what God says, to listen all ears, when he speaks out and voices an opinion.

Morality in this light is unconditional submission to God's commands, even when these commands may seem unmoral to mere rational understanding. It is quite different from a system of demands made by man on himself, which he undertakes to fulfill under his own power and of his own volition. In this regard again Christianity exhibits its fixation on an early phase of human self-understanding, a phase in which rules actually derived through a combination of moral urge and social expediency are projected outward and taken to be supernaturally ordained. Human custom and lawgiving merge into a moral concept and this concept merges with the will of God. Ethics here is the sum of all those conventions in force at the moment when society is primed to lay down ethical principles. As such this system contains no moral principles of universal import, but rather prescripts the regulation of behavior in detail.

A prescriptive ethic always restricts development and makes for moral crisis, since it cannot be adjusted to new forms of living. An ethic of this nature is continually having to face a decision as to whether it is better to hold fast to inherited norms with their pretensions of absolute validity, and thus condemn all change as heresy, or to affirm change and speak out in favor of the "overthrow of all custom." In the New Testament the purely legalistic ethic of Judaism was, to be sure, discarded in favor of a proclama-

tion of universal moral requirements, but the unworkableness of
these new demands was such that the Ten Commandments type
of morality of the Old Testament remained effective for Christianity. However, it is hardly surprising, in view of the fact that man is
not a creature who remains the same at all times and places, that
a mode of behavior laid down by the Jews 1200 years or so before
Christ should not always meet the needs of 20th-century European
man.

A traditionalist and anthropocentric type of man lies concealed
in Christianity's static and theocentric metaphysic. Its inability to
see man as a multilayered, constantly changing creature leads to a
narrowing of the consciousness of self, a restriction of it to the
surface layer of the human personality—the part of it, in short,
which constitutes what is called man's character. The consciousness
of self, therefore, is a pure ego-consciousness, which entangles man
inextricably in the mechanisms of his "attributes." When man is
identified with his character in this fashion, he becomes the victim
of the constant fluctuations of the ego-level. It is not mere chance,
therefore, that in Western civilization man is hounded throughout
his lifetime by ceaseless unrest and is chronically unable to attain
inner equilibrium and a sense of order. What he lacks is a point
outside himself from which vantage he can take objective measure
of himself.

It was psychoanalysis that first revealed the process-like automatism of the character. However, so far psychoanalysis has yet to
take the decisive step of separating the consciousness of self from
the consciousness of the ego. Nonetheless, signs are increasing
that the West is on the brink of learning from the experience of
the East in this regard. A possibility may yet be found of uniting
the techniques of depth psychology and meditation, thus at least
releasing European man from the unrest and superficiality caused

by his imprisonment in the ego. Just as a secure and pacific social order is the proper frame for man optimally to realize himself, the harmonizing of the ego is a prerequisite if man is to catch sight of his human potentialities at all. The Christian theory which teaches that man is imprisoned in his sinful, creature-like ego has caused the deeper insight into self to be so thoroughly forgotten that even today the methods of self-immersement practiced in east Asia for thousands of years seem to Western thought like trickery or the devil's work.

If, however, Western man, despite his enforced blindness, has preserved some degree of self-regard and self-trust, some feeling for his own measure, for this he has the legacy of antique philosophy, and his own pre-Christian history, to thank. Wherever in European history a humanist approach to the world has arisen, it has sprung from a profoundly "heathen" feeling. The knight without fear or blame, the gentilhomme, the gentleman, the heroic prototypes of the masses and of polite society, the ideals of tolerance and fair play—none of these guiding images and virtues are of Christian provenance. Christianity has been able to hold its own with these testimonials of natural humanity only by unflinching accommodation. Characteristic of European humanism is the fact that it must make its way as best it can in direct opposition to the image of man provided by prevailing belief. From this conflict arises the schizophrenia of the Western spirit, and from it, too, the unparalleled tension and diversity of forms of Western culture. A theocentric and ecstatic ethic fails man's natural humanity, and for this very reason compels him to strain his spiritual and intellectual powers to the utmost.

Ethical theory based on the wisdom of pantheist and romantic sages is quite different from the Christian ethic of love of God and renunciation. In Christianity the ideal image is the wise man who forsakes the world so he can devote his undivided attention to the completion of the self. But when this withdrawal occurs the very factor which makes man human is negated: his socially and historically bound existence. Modern man would go to pieces in a life of reverie, so thoroughly is he disinclined to such a form of existence. The wise man who goes off into the desert or the forest represents a mutation, a special kind of personality able to function apart from the rest of the human species and its life-system. The superman is periously close to the monster. And because of this, failure to appreciate religious genius can be a form of self-protection.

Existence is not a uniform structure, nor does it strive for uniformity. On the contrary, it is quantitatively and qualitatively multiform, multilayered. And it is precisely in this multiplicity of differentiation and structure that it finds fulfillment and gets meaning. Therefore, anyone who, in the midst of living, tries to complete life by contemplating it in terms of discovering uniformities in depth is actually engaged in the pointless task of obviating the world, of doing away with what, in fact, is most important in it. The misled contemplative places a false construction on things and relationship systems. Whereas actually they belong to the world, he wrenches them out of it, from them making categories that lie outside the world and history. This he does in order to confirm their "worthlessness." This kind of wisdom, which fancies itself superior to human dimension, does not enhance and complete the human scheme, but surrenders before it.

One of the avenues of escape used by Western man from the unacceptability of the dualist Christian metaphysic is flight into mystic and pansophist religious ideas, that is, ideas of tidally large application. This expedient, to be sure, expresses a true instinct for the monistic structure of the universe, but one gone astray into antirealism. It winds up with an image of the world foreign to form and order, one which of necessity negates the limitedness and elaborate structuration of reality, since after all its whole purpose is to get directly in touch with the unlimited, the unarticulated and the absolute. An obsession of this kind with totality, the universal, always inclines to overlook the structures conditioning the world, and by extension to deem the specifically human, with its rational, social and moral aspects, as of trivial importance. It represents an attempt to reverse the world process of becoming and to flatten out the contours of existence, with all its countless forms, qualities and systems, into the uniformity of an all-embracing being realizable here and now in existence. Pseudo-wisdom of this sort prematurely and erroneously equates the absolute with the negation of the relative, the essential with the negation of the existential and the eternal with the negation of the temporarily governed, all this without realizing that existence is not abolished by negating the elements of existence, but merely mishandled and its problems scamped. Quite true, mysticism and pansophism, the pretension to universal knowledge, do eliminate a separation into two worlds, one given over to the devil and sin, the other to God and redemptive promise. However, the mundane and real, thought of as they are in this context as surface and husk of the divine immanence in all things, still remain illusory and devoid of meaning. As a result a new dualism slips into the picture: a partition of the world into the meaningful and the unmeaning, the valuable and the valueless, the eternal and the transitory.

The true sage knows that it is senseless to play being against existence, and that the kind of life suitable for a saint, if carried over into society, would destroy rather than pacify it. On this account it is out of weakness, not strength, that the false philosopher is driven to put on an air of melancholy superiority when he con-

templates mundane things. Every time he finds that his intellectual
and moral strength are not great enough to move men to action in
the world, to create a human order, he draws back into the dark,
unfathomable and universal. Then, when he is forced to give up
his claim to being a thinker, he makes himself out to be a specialist
in the esoteric, an intuitionist, a cosmosophist. When he is unable
to do justice to the problems of society, he says defensively that
after all he is not political-minded, or that he is above politics.
When he cannot manage his personal life, he turns the conver-
sation to the fullness and depth of his soul. He pretends to be
above things, he fancies himself able to reconcile the realities that
harshly jostle each other in actual space with the ideals of an only
apparent world. While Guelfs and Ghibellines are busy cutting
each other's heads off, he muses thoughtfully, emptily on the fool-
ishness and contrariety of the human race. While men are striving
desperately to have the right recognized and make it prevail, he
sits back to enjoy a *frisson* of metaphysical intuition.

There is, too, another and very similar form of evading responsibility in human affairs. This is by retreat into artistic pleasure, by
assuming, as so many art-lovers do, that the esthetic has value as
a way to knowledge and release. Music in particular, for the devotees who give themselves up unreservedly to it, gives the illusion
that in its mood of profoundly empathic surrender all the problems
of existence can be solved. But in truth such exaltations only
momentarily assuage the cares of every day. It is a wise move greatly
to mistrust a certain kind of art, artistic enjoyment and art interpretation—the kind, in brief, which seeks to create the delusion
that man can join the chosen few who are wise and complete
merely on the basis of connoisseurship and enthusiasm, without any
other effort. But any art which professes to be a sort of substitute
for humanity, which tries to give the impression that the ability

to practice and enjoy it are signs of superior intellectual and moral qualification, is trying to pass counterfeit coin. The practice and enjoyment of art are means of representing and experiencing the world, not a way to become good or wise.

To forgo sharing, through participation in its decisions, in the maintenance and reinforcement of human order is not a virtue, but a form of neglect, of shirking. It simply does not lie within the capacity of the man who lives among men to step at will out of the continuum of society and history, in such a way that his decision not to make decisions should paradoxically prove influential on the relationships of this life. Doing this sort of thing violates the social order. It is a way of refusing to lift a hand for the human scheme, though it is man's specific obligation, and his alone, to use his given abilities to support this scheme. Anyone who introduces the metaphysical principle of the resolution of opposites into a world teeming with antithesis merely tends to erase the given order of appearance and reduce it to featureless pulp, a formlessness in which the human factor, like all else, can find no point of departure to develop from. Paradises and golden ages are meaningless and phantom projections. They assume the existence of an ideal world which, though made out of the same elements as the real world, obeys laws which would annihilate these same elements existentially.

The lion that eats grass instead of the lamb is not a lion at all, but a sheep in a lion's skin. A proclivity for eating lambs, as long as lions exist, will continue to be part and parcel of leoninity. And should a lion perchance eat grass, he will not be higher among his lion kind, but simply a sadly misguided, ass of a beast. A man who does not strive to make use of all his intellectual and moral abilities to improve the life of humankind, but instead excessively concerns himself with heightening his cosmic emotions, like the aforementioned lion is not a higher type of man, but a misguided one. Anyone who seeks to establish the essential identity of all things must cancel out not only the laws and conditions impressed on these things, but the very things themselves, the two being inseparable. Take man out of his social and historical setting, and he must either be forced back into the animal or vegetative, or elevated to the divine. No form of appearance in this world can be divorced from the form of existence to which it is attached. Existential form is not something extra, something added, an order imposed from above, but the thing itself.

The irrationalist systems composed of supposedly accepted absolutes, when they undertake to express the absence of meaning, as they claim, in all forms of order laid down for and by man, tend to develop a method of arriving at what to the intellect is meaningless and inconceivable by means of the absurd. The classical example of this kind of double-talk are the "Koans" of Zen Buddhism, that is, rather brief and simply stated questions of a puzzling nature admitting of no logical answer. (A traditional Koan: "What is the sound of one hand clapping?") The shockingly contradictory and unintelligible formulas of this philosophy of absurdity are intended to expose the merely relative validity of rational and moral effort. To be sure, to the extent that Zen is used as a method to ascertain the deeper reality of things otherwise hidden and distorted by our conventional habits of thought and speech, it is an excellent means of forfending all forms of shallow positivism. However, in the hands of the uninitiated, a procedure of this nature, visiting irony as it does on our whole conceptual habit, and seeing everything in a relative light, can easily become an occasion for considering all reasonableness banal and all morality second-rate. The unsophisticated mind, under the disturbing influence of images at once profound and nonsensical, the teaching and thera-

peutic aim of which is not appreciated, arrives in dealing with the
problems of existence at the dangerous conclusion that true intellectual sovereignty lies in rejecting all objective experience as merely
apparent and illusory. Once this step has been taken, it is no
longer necessary to find solutions for real, immediate problems at
all. Robbing them of their urgency by a species of intellectual
magic is deemed accomplishment enough. Misled in this fashion,
there are enthusiasts, whole sects of them, who expect that world
peace and the solution of all political and social conflict can be
achieved by the mere avowal of some pacifist or altruistic program,
or by some kind of mystical-magical manipulation ensuring, as
they imagine, the true and opportune attainment of the absolute.

Into this category falls the West's erroneous longing and search
for the wisdom of the East. True enough, east Asia has much to
teach us. The thinkers of Asia much earlier and much more clearly
than those of the West realized that the nature of the world is a
universal continuum embodying many spheres of existence, the
one developing out of the other and all interrelated, and that the
human person must be understood as a multilayered process con-
sisting of many causally linked subprocesses fulfilled in relation to
an impersonal core that reaches down into the realm of being. But
the Asian's exclusive concentration on finding ways and means of
escaping from existence has led to a failure to recognize that human
existence in itself has meaning and value, and that being cannot
possibly have, so to speak, committed itself to existence only later
to ignore itself in this guise. We are drawing ever closer to a return
to being, and it is a good thing for human insight to keep this
central fact in mind. At the same time there can be no doubt that
the "advice" of being, as it discharges us into existence, cannot be
other than to stand by this existence, according to our peculiar
mode.

Because of this preoccupation with escape from existence, Asia has neglected the two great fields of Western accomplishment, science and history, by which latter term we mean a vital awareness of belonging within a historical process, here and now. And that it is a question of simple neglect, and not of premeditation, is evidenced by the fact that the Asians are now finding themselves constrained to adopt the scientific and history-conscious modes of Western thought. In actual fact, philosophical speculation was pursued so intensively in Asia that no energy or interest was left for objective, physical investigation. In sum, the Asian thinkers have bypassed the circumstance that intensive preoccupation with ways to individual release does not exempt them from the obligation of making man's collective life as efficiently organized and regulated as possible. This inability to accept reality, indeed, an aversion to it, characteristic of Asian peoples, has been a tragic mistake, the results of which have been centuries of social immaturity and misery. This lag is visible to this day as fumbling attempts are made to catch up in decades with countries of the West whose material progress has taken centuries to accomplish. All these Asian peoples will have to free themselves from the idea that Western science, technology and politics are products that are being forced upon them by a particular historical constellation.

No people, over the long run, can get along without making use of their powers of reason. Typical is the way the revolution in China, in its beginning stages, exactly like the Bolshevist revolution before it, widely overshot the mark. Faced with repairing the neglect of centuries, the Chinese passionately embraced ideas of progress and civilization, meanwhile relegating traditional virtues and values to the dust-bin. In Gandhi, on the other hand, just the opposite was the case. Gandhi had unlimited trust in the Indian people's ability to resist being overrun by Western forms of life.

Gandhi confused emancipation from British imperialism with emancipation from the necessity of having to come to terms with democratic and industrial world revolution. Not until Pandit Nehru's generation came into power was it generally realized that no amount of moral superiority on India's part could spare the new country from active participation in social and industrial upheaval.

In sum, Asia has much to learn from us, even as we have from her. In turning to reality, the struggle to understand and control which the West must thank for its greatness, the East has taken the first step toward realizing its human potential, a theme which cannot be neglected if the Asian is ever to achieve a well-rounded development of his capacities. Moreover, not until the Western World has recognized the inherent limitations of Asian insights, at least as known to date, can their assimilation, necessary and desirable though it is, be fruitfully carried out. In any event, nothing less than the East's affirmation of the will to investigate reality methodically and to impress order on it, the faculty so highly developed in the West, can enable Asia to free itself from the crippling tendency to become lost in the visionary and exalted, the esoteric and mystagogic, which hitherto has made so much of its philosophical effort fruitless and unpalatable.

In the currently incipient and unavoidable phase of historicity and sociality, the world-blindness of pansophist idealism is ultimately more to be feared than a retrogression toward the subhuman. In actual fact this kind of idealism sets the stage for just such a retrogression. More important, however, an error of this nature is not easy to detect. Barbarian attempts to reduce the historical process to a question of biology or sociology are immediately apparent to everybody. But an idealistically couched indifferentism, far from being understood in all its unfortunate connotations, may very well be revered and accorded high value.

Nevertheless, however kindhearted and amiable it may appear to be on the surface, such idealism represents a false humanity. Ideas supposed to be outside time, space and causal necessity can never serve as a standard for what happens, or should happen, in the world of here and now to us and through us. Every pansophism, every form of pretension to universal knowledge which tries to unfold in the world proper tends to lull to sleep those very abilities which make for activity and expressiveness in the human sphere— sympathy, judgment, the readiness to make decisions. The resolution of opposites, the smoothing out of differences, the reduction to bagatelles of rational and human values—all this has nothing to offer the man of action. His concern, on the contrary, should be to make human values obligatory and attainable in a world that so far is only partially humanized. Anyone who tries to set himself above the world of things succeeds only in lending support to the nonhuman, or the as yet not quite human, world, for the reason that his preoccupation is not to carry along the organization of human existence, but to abolish all such organization, including its human factor. To behave in this manner, as if the essential identity of all things were an existential problem of superior interest, to treat all realms of existence as if differences were no more than illusory husks, this destroys the specificity of the very realm of existence to which man belongs.

Life as lived within society and history must be understood as the sole setting in which humanity can be realized. On the other hand, life's specific structure provides no excuse for projecting it into infinity, or for thinking of its values as absolute. However long eternity may be, before we enter this world or after we leave it, as long as we are here and alive, we must live, and are bound to seek communication, with the super- and the extra-human using our given talents as best we can. Nevertheless contempt for history and science is no more wrong than thinking that the most important thing in this life is to investigate scientifically and act efficiently. Metaphysics does not annul physics or history, but neither is metaphysics a kind of physics or history on a celestial plane.

Each sphere created by nature has its own meaning and its own laws, and the existence of one sphere does not diminish the value or the reality of another. Stones justify their existence by having endurance and weight, stars theirs by revolving in their courses, emitting light and alternately expanding and contracting. Similarly, the legality and rightness of the human world arise from the simple fact that they exist as such. To be gifted with intelligence is equivalent with being charged to make use of this intelligence, really to know and accomplish something with this gift. With the aid of intelligence we realize an essential part of our total nature and through it are led to the limits of our human powers. The means by which knowledge is made possible is the same means used in grasping that there is something that goes beyond us. This limitation, incidentally, applies equally to feeling and understanding, intuition and rationality. Good and bad likewise are categories which make sense only in the world of man. But in this world of man their importance is serious indeed, for to exist meaningfully on the human level, man must not live vegetatively, zoologically or spiritually, but, very simply, as a human being.

14

BY WAY OF CONCLUSION

THE BASIC LAWS of the Western democracies guarantee freedom of religion and of conscience. Meanwhile, in all these countries there are groups, large and small, of citizens who either do not belong to any Christian community at all, or are members of a group that is admittedly non-Christian. Other than these people there are many church members, the number of whom can only be guessed at, who, while included in Christian statistics, are not Christians in fact. But even if we take only unbelievers and those committed to non-Christian forms of belief, both of which groups are quite conscious of their non-Christianity, we have a total many times greater than the ratio of dissidence officially listed. The question now arises why it is that all these non-Christians fail to exercise their freedom of religion and of conscience, and why at least some of them, having dared to leave the Church, should not have become organized minorities. The only answer can be that in spite of man's "inalienable rights," non-Christian ideological convictions, unlike deviations from prevailing political opinion, dare not be openly proclaimed. For this state of affairs neither the state nor the Christian churches are responsible, but that anonymous, yet omnipotent censor called "public opinion."

Naturally cases are always coming up where the constitutional rights of the unchurched citizen are rudely ignored or limited by organs of the state, or menaced by virtue of the claims to authority of ecclesiastic institutions. But the real and decisive curb on conscience (originally made possible by the encroachment into private life of church and state) is the inhibiting pressure brought to bear on the human conscience by society itself, which suppresses everything tending to cast doubt upon its claim and wish to appear as Christian, or at any rate as aspirantly Christian. When opinions or interests appear that are strongly opposed to the conviction that everybody must be Christian, all organizations, groups, associations unite in a solid front of disapprobation. Even liberals and socialists, erstwhile leaders in the fight for freedom of the spirit, are put out when reminded, in this general connection, of their heroic role. They, too, rush to fall in line with the general outcry against any such "political misuse of the religious issue," and let it be known that they, too, take their stand "on the common ground of Christian principles."

This collective zeal at every opportunity to avow "Christian principles" leads to a form of ideological speech-control marked by a degree of uniformity and effectiveness that no totalitarian propaganda minister could possibly achieve. The few intellectuals rash enough (and who find an opportunity) freely to proclaim their agnosticism are treated as macabre outsiders more to be pitied than condemned. Their deviation is so thoroughly felt to be a shameful betrayal of ideals which are highly held by common consent that blockheadedness or eccentricity are the mildest defects ascribed to them. The most widespread reaction, however, is to equate any public avowal of "godlessness" with being a communist. Only on paper is it possible to express beliefs contrary to traditional ideas, public opinion having generated a conformism equivalent to a ban on "religious" and ideological discussion.

Although today devotion to the real Christian creed is limited to a minority, a great many admitted dissidents even now are still not quite sure whether their unbelief might not be a kind of spoilsport attitude or a breach of trust. Ever since the days when Hitler and Stalin brought non-Christian ideas into bad odor, unbelievers have learned how to conceal their inability to believe in Christianity as if it were some sort of disgraceful stigma, and they take great pains to avoid public utterance against Christianity's claim to power and leadership. In view of the fact that the authors of all the unmistakable evil meted out to us during decades recently past openly boasted of their godlessness, it is no easy matter to resist the impression that the good must by the same token lie in a return to belief in God. So deeply has the identification of being un-Christian with being inhuman been impressed on the general consciousness that everyone feels it is his duty, if not to go to church or to trouble his head over religious questions, at any rate to declare his willingness to support all efforts favoring the use of Christianity's cultural blessings. Under these circumstances it is also understandable that the general alacrity in point of promoting Christian programs and organizations, far from being diminished by one's own private sickness of doubt, is in fact increased by it. We are currently witnessing a most curious performance, in which contemporary man professes himself to be a Christian with a vehemence that increases in direct proportion to his loss of faith. The farther his ideology and mode of living stray from Christianity, the more implacably he declares himself for his lost faith.

There are, to be sure, certain illusions the wholesale destruction

of which would do more harm than good. Nonetheless, the myth
that the Western World is Christian in character, or that the
Christian character should be preserved, does not belong—as we
trust we have by now made abundantly clear—among them. The
claim that Western man is Christian man, or should and must
become Christian again, is a coercive notion which could serve to
destroy all self-trust and humanist power of resistance once it has
become generally self-evident that non-Christianity is a condition
no longer to be avoided. Either we are convinced that human
values can be conceived and defended without the aid of Christianity, or we must get ready to capitulate. Seen from the standpoint
of mass illusion, in terms of which the West is currently trying to
wage the "war of ideas," our side, over the long run, is neither
capable of withstanding the onslaught of totalitarian ersatz religion, nor of controlling the manifold forms of crisis which the age
of the industrialized masses has brought in its wake.

We have seen how all the ideological and existential aberrations,
the true nature of which is actually more hidden than revealed in
such catchwords as "collectivism," "materialism," "nihilism," "disintegration," etc., are phenomena related to the collapse of the
Christian West, decomposition products of a breakdown of belief.
They are not (as so many diagnosticians seem to assume) a sickness introduced by foreign barbarians from the East. Since, funda-
mentally, the collapse of the pre- and anti-scientific world image has
been wrought by an irreversible process of enlightenment, and is
not at all a curable spiritual indisposition, the actual alternatives
are not giving up to barbarism on the one hand or a return to
belief on the other, but barbarism on the one hand and on the
other progress in the direction of a new and believable ideology and
ethic. The last is the only valid alternative and can no longer be
denied post-Christian man.

It is quite understandable that the Church should make the effort of ensuring good public relations and try to strengthen its position at every turn. However, it should be obligatory for all associations and institutions whose function it is to serve society as a whole to keep apart from special interests, meanwhile responding to collective dreams of wishfulness and finding out what contemporary man's thinking and doing are really like. But as matters stand public opinion is a collective instrument for the suppression of uncomfortable facts and for the curtailment of freedom of religion and conscience. All that has been discovered by social science and the liberal arts, all the material accumulated by inquiry into deep-reaching changes in our image of the world and feeling for life, all this is made the object of indignation and admonition, and resentfully preyed upon by reactionary *feuilletonistes*. The concept of "human responsibility," which everybody claims to know all about, turns out to be a crass affair of approving and publicizing all opinions that happen to have a good current circulation, or which fall in line with wishful thinking, while at the same time giving short shrift to all deviations from this blanket reaction. The arbitrary idea that the Christian West must be defended and saved seems to have made any factually correct interpretation of events impossible, even when these events unroll before our very eyes.

But despite all these maneuvers to deceive others and ourselves, it is becoming increasingly difficult to reconcile the actual practice of modern life, its actual forms of behavior, with Christian principles ostensibly unique in their validity and ostensibly recognized as valid by all. We have already indicated how the civilized citizen's claim to political and intellectual autonomy has never been compatible with the authoritarian structure of the Christian image of the world. It is quite impossible to effect a compromise between the idea that man is lost without the intervention of redeemers, prophets and priests and the conviction that man's fate lies in his own hands alone. The only possible end result of a way of life that says A, means B and does C is hopeless contradiction. Since the Christian churches are much more keenly aware of the drift away from them than public opinion is prepared to admit, they feel constrained to undertake experiments in reform and accommodation to check the process of de-Christianization. Attempts are made to revalorize Christianity by drawing as close as possible to "reality" and "everyday life." The leading confessions organize mass demonstrations, conventions, seminars, discussions, all sorts of gatherings at which people "get down to brass tacks" and "look the facts squarely in the face."

But all that is accomplished by these activities is the compilation of an inventory, a listing of the actual problems. At one Protestant church conference the theme was "Marriage—A Pain in the Neck." The consensus of opinion on this important, if rather unconventionally expressed subject, was that marriage is not really a union between two people, a partnership or contract, but an institution laid down by God, and as such indissoluble. Now, this way of looking at marriage may be perfectly self-evident to a Christian believer, but it certainly misses the mark with people—who also have needs and scruples—who no longer believe in "institutions laid down by God." What possible diagnostic or therapeutic value for the "unbeliever" can such a discussion have when it does not even refer to the social, psychological and intellectual causes of the marriage crisis, when it assumes from the start that any form of behavior not consistent with Christian ideas must be based on a "fall from grace," which of course means that it can be remedied only by a "return to God." It is as if the whole business could be straightened out by a mere act of good will, as if such a spiritual act, were it possible, would immediately have secular repercussions.

What justification is there, moreover, for assuming that changes in public morals, as evidenced in the ever widening discrepancy between prevailing convention and actual behavior, must necessarily be a sign of moral decay? Could not these changes be the first manifestations of new ideals? What arguments can Christianity really offer to prove that it is immoral when two people, after mature deliberation and reasonable trial, conclude that the psychological health of both can be preserved only if one leaves the other's bed and board? Will individual dignity or civilized marriage in general actually be thrown into jeopardy if man sets up a standard freeing human beings from dependencies that make for deformity? Is it immoral to want to help every human being develop a serene and secure character?

We know today that in his very brief history man has created so many different workable forms of coexistence that it is utterly impossible to support any such claim that this or that convention, and no other, is "absolutely moral." Moreover, as it turns out, those changes to which "the right way of living" is susceptible are directly related to broad social and civilizational changes. No one, unless he is adamantly determined to be deaf and blind, can fail to observe that we are living in a period in which profound upheavals are taking place below the surface of traditional value systems.

The motto adopted by the church conference cited above was "Make Your Peace with God." Thus, all the "ticklish questions" on the agenda were answered before the performance even got under way. Whatever errors and weaknesses may be keeping man on the hop are simply caused by a mulish refusal to believe in the speculations of Christian theology. A pastoral system which, in a period marked by decay of belief, tries to persuade people into thinking that their existence can be made orderly and meaningful only by a return to the faith, ends up as a massive pressure on the collective conscience and comes pretty close to demanding that all humane ideals and considerations, should the "unbeliever" prove incorrigible, be thrown to the winds. Christians know very well that humanly worthwhile changes in a way of life have nothing at all to do with religious commitment. They should, therefore, scorn to heighten modern man's confusion by equating decline of religion with decline of humanity. The sole interest of the various churches and confessions, whether dealing with believers, doubters or unbelievers, is to get one single point across: that their particular religious postulates are uniquely worthy of belief. Now, if they succeed in doing this, they need worry no more about the state of opinions and morals which they happen to feel are Christian and inalienable. And if they do not succeed in achieving conviction, well, they should clearly realize that the decisive basis for success was simply lacking.

We know that there are many Christians who are open-minded and who interest themselves in contemporary needs. There are Christians, we realize, who give help whether the person helped goes to church or not. Even so, how can we hope that the correctness of theological speculation is guaranteed by its adherents' altruism? Or that acceptance of ridiculous propositions can be facilitated if theologians become football players, or show an interest in jazz or abstract art? Among questionable experiments of this nature likewise fall attempts to give the Bible a new look, meanwhile heaping praise on it as if it were some sort of bestseller teeming with sensation. No sensible person will deny that many of the happenings described in the Old and New Testaments are based on actual historical events. But why should this be taken as proof that the speculative material in the Bible is also true? This is a secret privy only to those who make such assertions.

It is certainly the prerogative of the Christian churches to choose their own methods of winning conviction. All that we claim is the right to subject these heuristic arguments to untrammeled analysis. It strikes us as intolerable that in a civilization claiming to be the home of intellectual freedom the non-Christian must behave like a thief in the night. Let the non-Christian be free to think as he wishes and voice his opinions without hindrance. We make this plea not because we imagine it is a matter of life and death that everybody should be indulged in point of voicing opinions whenever he wishes, but because we believe that a clarification of our spiritual situation depends on an open discussion of all problems arising from the existence of the "unbeliever." The menacing crises of our time can be dealt with only if all people who are forever estranged from Christianity are helped to the knowledge that their estrangement neither relieves them from the responsibility, nor denies them the possibility, of seeking after a meaning for their existence. If it were only a case of having to repel Christianity's claim to a monopoly on truth, we would have been spared the effort of this discussion, since that claim has been refuted often and convincingly enough. But we are concerned with the much weightier fact that the uncritical assumption of the equivalence of "Christianity," "religion" and "true humanity" prevents post-Christian man from recognizing and doing something about his metaphysical and human needs.

As long as public opinion in the West insists that the world can be saved only by accepting Christian postulates as true, the period of unbelief will be greatly prolonged and ever new generations will be driven to cynicism, superficiality and stupidity.